STUDENT'S BOOK
with Interactive eBook

4

CEFR
B2

TH!NK

SECOND EDITION

Herbert Puchta,
Jeff Stranks &
Peter Lewis-Jones

CAMBRIDGE
UNIVERSITY PRESS

CONTENTS

C Conversations; Personality; Using *should*; Career paths; Decisions; Permission
D A change of lifestyle?; Reporting verbs; Negative adjectives; Another country; Changes; Regrets: *I wish … / If only …*

PRONUNCIATION	THINK!	SKILLS
Dipthongs: alternative spellings	**Train to Think:** Thinking rationally	**Reading** Article: Surviving for seven weeks Article: How to survive in the wilderness **Writing** A diary page about an experience **Listening** Radio show: *Exams advice*
Phrasal verb stress	**Train to Think:** Distinguishing fact from opinion **Values:** Learning from other cultures	**Reading** Article: Getting to work Blog: A Brazilian adventure **Writing** An informal email **Listening** Radio quiz about migration in nature
B2 First for Schools practice		
Adding emphasis	**Train to Think:** Changing your opinions	**Reading** Blog: An embarrassing dad Website page: To sharent or not to sharent **Writing** An essay about parenting **Listening** Podcast about a hero dad
Pronouncing words with *gh*	**Train to Think:** Lateral thinking **Values:** Appreciating creative solutions	**Reading** Article: A big change for artists Web post: A problem on *Your answers here* **Writing** A story beginning: *'I had no idea what to do.'* **Listening** Talking heads – thinking imaginatively
B2 First for Schools practice		
The schwa /ə/ sound	**Train to Think:** The PMI strategy	**Reading** Article: A digital detox Article: Great success for teenage teachers: When silver surfers get connected **Writing** Instructions **Listening** A conversation about an invention
Linked words with /dʒ/ and /tʃ/	**Train to Think:** Exaggeration **Values:** Doing good	**Reading** Email: Comic Con Article: CoderDojo Coolest Projects International **Writing** An essay about social media **Listening** Podcast: *Friendships*
B2 First for Schools practice		
Intonation: encouraging someone	**Train to Think:** Learning to see things from a different perspective	**Reading** Blog: My takes on life, the universe and everything Website page: Quotations for worriers **Writing** A short story ending: 'Every cloud has a silver lining' **Listening** Radio show: *Silver Linings*
Weak forms with conditionals	**Train to Think:** The 'goal-setting' checklist **Values:** Lists	**Reading** Book review: *The Checklist Manifesto* by Atul Gawande Blog: Elisa's list blog **Writing** An essay: A wonder of the natural world **Listening** A conversation about bucket lists
B2 First for Schools practice		
Linking: intrusive /w/ and /j/	**Train to Think:** Jumping to a hasty conclusion	**Reading** Presentation: Making difficult decisions Quiz: What kind of a friend are you? **Writing** An article for the school magazine **Listening** A radio programme about life choices
Linking: omission of the /h/ sound	**Train to Think:** Recognising the source of a statement	**Reading** Magazine article: Fake news Article: The Secret Paparazzo **Writing** A magazine article about an interview with a well-known person **Listening** An interview with a foreign correspondent
B2 First for Schools practice		
Stress on modal verbs for speculation	**Train to Think:** Spotting flawed arguments	**Reading** Article: A mission to Mars Blog: Top four space films of all time **Writing** A report about a problem on a school trip **Listening** Podcast about space tourism
Linking: intrusive /r/	**Train to Think:** Exploring hidden messages **Values:** Human activity and the natural world	**Reading** Article: Saving great discoveries! Article: Explorers: a friend to the native people: Cândido Rondon **Writing** A short biography **Listening** A talk about discovering new species

B2 First for Schools practice

WELCOME

A WHAT A STORY!

A lucky pilot

1 W.01 **Complete the conversation with the verbs from the list in the correct tense. Then listen and check your answers.**

add | carry | ~~crash~~ | destroy | dive | end
find | hit | manage | pull | scream | set

Mike So, did you see that story about the plane that [0] ____*crashed*____ into the ocean?

Finn No, I didn't. What happened?

Mike Well, this guy [1] ________ off from Florida in his plane – a small one, only one engine – to go to New Orleans.

Finn Wow – that's a long way.

Mike Right, and it's usually too far for a plane like that, but he had [2] ________ extra fuel tanks. However, after he had begun his journey, he realised he didn't have enough fuel to [3] ________ on flying, so he radioed New Orleans and told them that he was in trouble. He told them he had to land the plane in the sea.

Finn In the sea?

Mike Yes, there was a fishing boat not far away that was able to pick the pilot up. But here's the incredible thing – and you can see it in a video. The plane had a parachute, but it didn't work and the plane started to [4] ________ towards the sea! But then almost at the last minute, the parachute pulled the plane horizontal, just before it [5] ________ the water. The impact almost [6] ________ the plane.

Finn And the pilot?

Mike He was OK. He [7] ________ to get out of the plane and into a life raft from the fishing boat. Then the people from the fishing boat came and [8] ________ him out of the raft and took him to the ship. He wasn't injured, so he didn't [9] ________ up in hospital or anything. Now they're trying to [10] ________ out what went wrong.

Finn Wow – I'd have been so scared if I'd been in that plane. I'd have [11] ________ really loudly!

2 **Read the dialogue again. Answer the questions.**

1. Where was the plane flying to and from?
2. Why had the pilot added extra fuel tanks?
3. What did the pilot use to try to land the plane safely in the sea?
4. How was the pilot rescued?

Descriptive verbs

3 **Match the verbs with the definitions.**

1 demolish	a to hit very hard and break
2 dive	b to run away quickly
3 flee	c to go down quickly
4 grab	d to destroy completely
5 rage	e to shout loudly in a high pitch
6 scream	f to take hold of something quickly
7 smash	g to hit
8 strike	h to burn very fiercely

4 **Complete the sentences with the correct form of one of the verbs from Exercise 3.**

0 When the clock ____*struck*____ 12, I knew it was time to go home.
1 When war broke out, hundreds of people had to ________ the country.
2 I went back to my old school, but it wasn't there any more: it had been ________ .
3 I was late for the bus, so I just ________ my bag and ran to the bus stop!
4 The fire at the old factory ________ for over three hours.
5 She got really angry and ________ a plate against the wall.
6 They ________ but nobody heard them.
7 She ________ off the bridge and into the river.

Phrasal verbs

5 Complete the sentences from the dialogue on page 4. Then read again and check your answers.

1 The pilot ________________ from Florida in his plane to go to New Orleans.
2 The pilot wasn't injured so he didn't ________________ in hospital.
3 Now they're trying to ________________ what went wrong with the fuel calculations.

6 Choose the correct words.

1 My father's health has improved so much since he *gave up* / *ended up* smoking.
2 She wanted to get fit so she *gave up* / *took up* judo.
3 It's a bit of a problem, but I'm sure we can *sort it out* / *blow it out*.
4 If we *get on* / *carry on* walking this slowly, we won't get there before dark.
5 We're going to the big match tomorrow – I'm *looking forward to* / *looking into* it.
6 He's very tall and he's got red hair, so he really *stands out* / *looks out* in a crowd.
7 I got there really late because the bus *broke down* / *blew out*.
8 All the restaurants were closed, so we *took up* / *ended up* eating at a fast-food place.

Childhood memories

7 SPEAKING Work with a partner. What do you remember about your first visit to the cinema (e.g. who you went with, what the film was, etc.)?

8 Read this extract from an autobiography. Which of the things that you remember are mentioned?

Cinema paradise

I'm in my seventies now and I used to love going to the cinema when I was a kid. Back in the 1950s, there used to be a thing called Children's Matinee at the cinema in the town where we lived. It was wonderful! Every Saturday morning, the cinema would show films for kids – and only kids. They showed cartoons and cowboy films, adventure films, detective films and science fiction – everything that kids loved back then (and still do I guess!).

My brother used to take me – he was five years older than me. We'd always try to get there early so we could get seats in the front row, or at least, one or two rows back. The cinema sold ice cream and popcorn, and we would buy as much as we could, and then sit and watch the films while stuffing ourselves with food.

We loved the cartoons – we laughed a lot. Our favourite was always *Tom and Jerry* and we cheered when we saw the opening pictures. And then there were the adventure films. The plots were often terrible, and the dialogues, too, but we really didn't care – after all, we were kids! We used to boo the villains and cheer the heroes. Some kids used to throw popcorn at the screen when the villain came on – the cinema staff sometimes tried to stop us but usually they gave up! The ending was always completely predictable, of course – the hero always won – and we'd cheer like crazy when he did!

9 Read the extract again and answer the questions.

1 Who couldn't go to the Children's Matinees?
2 Who did the writer go with?
3 Why did they go early?
4 When did the children usually cheer?
5 When did they boo?

Elements of a story

10 Complete the text with words from the list.

characters | dialogue | ending | hero | plot | set | villain

I read a book last week called *Moscow Mystery*. It was a thriller – a kind of detective story. It is [1]________________ in Moscow. The [2]________________ of the story is a woman called Valentina, who helps many of the other [3]________________ to escape from a terrible situation – they have been kidnapped by a horrible old man called Nikolai, who's the [4]________________ of the story.
Anyway, the book's quite good. I thought the overall [5]________________ was quite exciting and it had a nice unexpected twist at the end.
(I won't tell you the [6]________________, though, in case you read the book yourself.) And I really liked the [7]________________, too – the conversations between the different characters sound like real people talking to each other. A good read – I'd recommend it.

11 SPEAKING In small groups, think of an example of each of these from a film or book.

1 a great hero
2 a terrifying villain
3 an amazing plot
4 a satisfying ending

Talking about past routines

12 Complete the sentences from the extract 'Cinema paradise'. Use *would* or *used to*.

1 I ____________ love going to the cinema as a kid.
2 My brother ____________ take me.
3 The hero always won, and we ____________ cheer when he did.
4 Some kids ____________ throw popcorn.

B AN UNCERTAIN FUTURE

Future plans

1 W.02 **Read the conversation. Put the phrases into the correct places. Then listen and check.**

when you leave school | get a good degree
to start a family | and then travel the world
then retire | before I think about settling down

Mum So, Jordan, have you thought about which university you want to go to yet?

Jordan I told you, Mum – I'm not so sure that I want to go to university.

Mum But if you [1] ____________________, you'll be guaranteed a secure future. You know, perhaps in ten years' time, you'll be managing a huge company!

Jordan But that's just it, Mum – I don't want to manage a big company, or a small company either. I don't want to spend 40 years doing that, [2] ____________________ and wonder where my life went. That's not the future I want – I think.

Mum Well, so what are you going to do [3] ____________________ then?

Jordan I'm not sure yet. Maybe work, save a bit of money [4] ____________________ for a few months, you know, get some life experience.

Mum Well, that won't do you much good. In this day and age, employers want people with work experience, not travel experience.

Jordan Well, maybe you're right, Mum. But even so, I want some time for myself [5] ____________________.

Mum There's nothing wrong with settling down. That's what your father and I did.

Jordan I know, Mum and that's fine – it was fine for you and Dad, back in the last century. But the world's different now and people have such different aims, ideas, everything!

Mum Yes, I suppose so. You're right.

Jordan But don't worry, Mum. I mean, I'd like [6] ____________________ at some point. So you'll be playing with your grandchildren one day – I hope.

Mum Well, I'm delighted to hear that, Jordan!

2 Mark the sentences T (true), F (false) or DS (doesn't say).

1 Jordan and his mum have talked about university before. ☐
2 Jordan's mother works for a big company. ☐
3 Jordan definitely wants to leave school and travel. ☐
4 Jordan's mother values work experience. ☐
5 Jordan would like to have children. ☐

Life plans

3 Complete the sentences with the words from the list.

career | degree | leave | promoted
retired | settled | start | travel

1 My plan was to ____________________ the world, but when I got to Italy, I loved it so much that I stayed.
2 I have no idea what to do when I ____________________ school.
3 She got an excellent ____________________ from Cambridge University.
4 He worked really hard and he got ____________________ to junior manager.
5 My uncle got ill when he was 55, so he ____________________ early.
6 A course in psychology is a good way to start a ____________________ in teaching.
7 My cousin has always moved from one place to another – he's never ____________________ down.
8 They feel they haven't got enough money yet to ____________________ a family.

4 SPEAKING **Work in pairs and discuss the questions. Then compare your answers in small groups.**

1 At what age can people leave school in your country? Do you think this is the right age? Why (not)?
2 At what age can people retire in your country? Is it the same for men and for women? Do you think this is the right age? Why (not)?
3 Is it important in your country to get a degree in order to have a good career? Why (not)?

Future continuous

5 Complete the sentences with the future continuous form of the verbs in the list.

listen | live | study | travel | wonder | work

In five years from now,

1 I'll ____________ the world.
2 I won't ____________ at home anymore.
3 I'll ____________ at university.
4 Some of my friends will ____________ for big international companies.
5 I'll ____________ to the same kind of music as I do now.
6 I'll still ____________ what to do with my life.

6 SPEAKING Work in pairs. Which of the statements from Exercise 5 are true for you? Which statements are true for your partner?

Future perfect

7 Complete the text with the future perfect form of the verbs in brackets.

Don't worry about Jordan. He'll be fine. By the time he's 20, he [1] ____________ (leave) school and he [2] ____________ (save) enough money to travel around the world. By the time he's 30, Jordan [3] ____________ (be) to every continent and [4] ____________ (decide) what he wants to do with his life. And by the time he's 40, Jordan [5] ____________ (settle) down and [6] ____________ (start) a family.

Being emphatic: *so* and *such*

8 Complete these sentences from the dialogue on page 6.

1 I'm not ____________ sure I want to go to university.
2 People have ____________ different aims, ideas, everything!

9 Make these statements more emphatic. Use *so* or *such*.

0 Leaving school is an important moment in your life.
Leaving school is such an important moment in your life.
1 Getting a job offer is an amazing feeling.
2 Spending money that you earned and saved is satisfying.
3 It's an awful waste of time to go travelling.
4 Deciding to settle down is a huge decision.
5 Worrying about their children is terrifying for parents.

10 Who do you think said the things in Exercise 9, Jordan or his mum? Write J or M in the boxes.

0 *M* 1 ☐ 2 ☐ 3 ☐ 4 ☐ 5 ☐

11 SPEAKING Work with a partner. Which of the statements in Exercise 9 do you (not) agree with?

Extreme adjectives

12 Look at the emphatic statements in Exercise 9 again. Find words which mean:

1 really scary ____________
2 really good ____________
3 really bad ____________
4 really big ____________

13 Write the words in the correct places.

brilliant | delighted | exciting | freezing
funny | hot | huge | interesting
miserable | scared | terrible | tiny

	Gradable adjective	Extreme adjective
1	bad	____________ / awful
2	good	fantastic / wonderful / ____________ / amazing
3	____________	fascinating
4	____________	terrified
5	____________	hilarious
6	happy	____________
7	sad	____________
8	____________	thrilling
9	big	____________ / enormous
10	small	____________ / minute
11	cold	____________
12	____________	boiling

14 Complete the dialogues with suitable extreme adjectives.

0 A The water's cold, isn't it?
B More than that – it's *freezing*!
1 A She's really funny, isn't she?
B Yes, she's ____________.
2 A That house is pretty small.
B Small?! It's ____________!
3 A I thought the film was really good, didn't you?
B Yes, I thought it was ____________.
4 A Wow! I was scared from beginning to end of that!
B Me, too! In fact, I was ____________!
5 A Was the concert really so bad?
B Yes, it was. It was ____________.

15 WRITING With a partner, write three more dialogues, using words from Exercise 13 that don't appear in Exercise 14.

C HOW PEOPLE BEHAVE

Conversations

1 W.03 **Listen and match the conversations to the pictures. Write 1–3 in the boxes.**

2 W.03 **Listen again. Complete the spaces with one word.**

Conversation 1

Dev What's the matter with you?

Megan Didn't you see? I held the door open for that elderly lady; I let her go through in front of me.

Dev Yes, I saw that. It was very thoughtful of you. Very [1]________________ .

Megan But she just walked past me and didn't say 'thank you'. She didn't even look at me! It's so [2]________________ , I think.

Dev Oh, you [3]________________ get so worked up. She was probably just thinking about something else.

Conversation 2

Milly Hi, Jack. Here are your headphones.

Jack My headphones! I've been looking for them. So, *you* took them?

Milly Yes – sorry, I should [4]________________ asked you, I know, but …

Jack Well, give them back. You're not [5]________________ to take my things without asking!

Milly OK. I'm sorry. But you don't have to be so [6]________________ , do you?

Conversation 3

Jason I'm so upset. I just heard that Paul, one of my best friends, is going to move to Canada.

Sarah Oh, that's a shame. But never [7]________________ , you've got other friends, haven't you?

Jason Yes, I know, but I'm going to miss him a lot. He's really fun to [8]________________ out with.

Sarah Well, you don't [9]________________ to lose touch with him, do you? You can Skype.

Jason That's right. And perhaps my parents will [10]________________ me go and visit him sometime.

3 SPEAKING **Work with a partner. What would you have said in these situations if you were:**

- Dev?
- Milly?
- Sarah?

Personality

4 SPEAKING **Work in pairs. Choose six of the adjectives. For each one, think of something that someone could say or do to show that quality.**

calm | cold | generous | lively | patient | polite | rude | selfish | shy | thoughtful | unfriendly | warm

If someone goes on holiday and brings you back a present – well, that's thoughtful.

Using *should*

5 **Write what you would say to reply to these people. Use a form of *should* and a personality adjective.**

0 I'm in a hurry – get out of my way.
Sure, but you shouldn't be so rude!

1 I heard you lost your pen, so I bought you a new one.
____

2 I was hungry, so I ate all the sandwiches, OK?
____

3 I had a big argument with my sister and told her I don't like her now.
____

4 I'd like to say hello to her, but I can't!
____

Career paths

6 SPEAKING What jobs do these people have? Discuss with a partner.

A

B

C

D

E

7 **Read the article quickly. Which of the jobs from Exercise 6 are mentioned?**

Home New posts Archives

TIPS FOR choosing a career

Choosing a career – something you might end up doing for the rest of your working life – isn't always easy, but equally, it doesn't have to be the agony that it turns into for some people. Here are our tips to help you make up your mind.

A Don't let other people tell you what to do!

There are always people who want you to become a doctor, or work in banking, or be a teacher. Listen to them, but remember it's your life and it's your decision, so be sure that you're the one who makes that decision!

B Consider what you think you're good at.

It's true that things like salary are important, but don't let financial considerations lead you down the wrong path. Follow your heart and your personality – if you're a very active person, don't choose an office job, even if the pay's good. In the same way, if you don't like work that involves paying lots of attention to detail, think long and hard before you decide to do something like applying to study engineering at university.

C Your first decision isn't forever.

Some lucky people get it right first time – they start a job, love it straight away and stick at it. But it isn't always like that, so remember – you're allowed to change your mind! Certainly, it's no good agonising for years: maybe your first job doesn't turn out the way you had wanted it to. That doesn't mean the right job for you isn't right around the corner!

D Do something of value.

Some people choose their career simply because they think they'll earn huge amounts of money (although the careers which pay the most – acting, writing, singing – also have millions of people who never make it to the top). OK, if that's what you want. But, generally, people get more satisfaction out of their career if they feel they are doing something valuable for others. It doesn't have to be charity work – it could be a job that helps other people in the community, like a carer for elderly people. Just don't forget that job satisfaction isn't only about money.

8 SPEAKING **Put the four tips (A–D) from the text in order to show how useful you think each one is (1 = most useful, 4 = least useful). Compare your ideas with a partner.**

Decisions

9 **Complete the questions with the words and phrases from the list.**

come to a | long and hard | make | make up | mind

1 What do you find it difficult to ________________ decisions about?
2 When do you think it's wrong to change your ________________ ?
3 Can you remember a time when you couldn't ________________ your mind about something?
4 Who do you talk to before you ________________ decision about something?
5 What kind of things do you think ________________ about before making a decision?

10 SPEAKING **Discuss the questions in Exercise 9 in pairs.**

Permission

11 **Complete the sentences with the correct form of *make*, *let* or *be allowed to*.**

1 You should never ________________ other people make decisions for you.
2 No employer can ________________ you work longer hours than the law permits.
3 My cousin's got a job where she ________________ work from home three days a week.
4 My grandfather left a job when the manager tried to ________________ him work late.
5 In the past, factories ________________ use children as workers – can you believe that?
6 This company ________________ its employees dress smartly from Monday to Thursday, but on Friday it ________________ them wear less formal clothes.

12 **Write sentences about your perfect job or career. Use *make* / *let* / *be allowed to* in some of your sentences.**

My ideal job lets me choose the times of day I work.

D NEW THINGS

A change of lifestyle

1 W.04 **Read and listen to the dialogue.**

1 Where are Tom and Maia?
2 Who doesn't want to be there? Why?

2 W.04 **Listen again and complete the gaps in the conversation.**

Tom You said it opened at eight o'clock.
Maia And I was wrong! I'm sorry. Don't be so [1]__________. It'll be open very soon.
Tom I already wish I hadn't come.
Maia Oh, come on, Tom. We [2]__________, didn't we? You said that you were fed up with your [3]__________ lifestyle.
Tom True. And then you [4]__________ me that the best thing to do was exercise.
Maia Right. And I [5]__________ you to come with me to the leisure centre, and you agreed, so here we are. We're going to work out for a while and then you'll feel great.
Tom I always feel [6]__________ wearing sports gear. I've got thin legs.
Maia Oh, stop complaining, Tom. There's nothing wrong with your legs.
Tom I asked you what I [7]__________ wear and you said shorts. But I look terrible!
Maia Look, no one here cares – everyone is completely unconcerned about what other people look like, they're all too busy doing exercise.
Tom That's completely untrue!
Maia Tom, I'm beginning to wish I [8]__________ invited you. Oh, look, it's opening. Come on then, let's go in and start.

3 **Answer the questions.**

1 Why has Tom agreed to try exercising?
2 Why is Tom not happy about wearing shorts?
3 Why, according to Maia, are people not worried about other people's appearance?
4 Why do you think Maia says: 'I'm beginning to wish I hadn't invited you'?

Reporting verbs

4 **Rewrite each sentence with the verbs in brackets.**

0 'Would you like to come to the match with me, Julie?' (invite)
He invited Julie to go to the match with him.
1 'The new baker in King Street is really good.' (recommend)
He __________
2 'No – I won't tell you the answers, James.' (refuse)
She __________
3 'I'm tired because I slept really badly last night.' (explain)
Mark __________
4 'OK, Mabel, I'll let you use my lipstick.' (agree)
She __________
5 'Go on, Boris – try the curry!' (encourage)
I __________

5 SPEAKING **Work in pairs. Tell your partner about the following things:**

1 a time someone persuaded you to do something
2 a book or film that someone recommended to you
3 something you would not encourage another person to do
4 something you agreed to do, but regretted

Negative adjectives

6 **Write the negative form of these adjectives.**

1 important __________
2 polite __________
3 possible __________
4 concerned __________
5 responsible __________
6 legal __________

7 **Complete the sentences using the negative form of an adjective in the list.**

~~expensive~~ | formal | happy
logical | patient | regular

0 I don't like spending money unnecessarily – I'm happy to buy *inexpensive* things.
1 I'll be ready in three minutes! Don't be so __________!
2 Something bad must have happened, she looks so __________.
3 You can wear what you want here. It's a really __________ place.
4 You want to travel in the summer holidays but you're not saving any money! That's just __________.
5 We never know when the next bus will come – the service is very __________.

Another country

8 **Read the blog. Which of the things in the photos does Jessica not talk about?**

Jessica's blog – *from Tokyo!*

Hi everyone,

Well, those of you who read my blog regularly know that I've moved – I'm now living in Tokyo: my parents got jobs here and they're on two-year contracts, so here we are. We got here about a month ago and we've found a place to live, so we're starting to feel a bit more settled.

It's so different here from home. Well, that's unsurprising, of course! For one thing, there are always so many people around, and for a country girl like me, who's used to peace and quiet, it isn't easy to deal with. Well, I guess I'll get used to it, but it might take a while! I just wish someone had told me in advance about the number of people on the trains to and from school! But I've made a resolution: I'm going to use my time spent travelling wisely – to learn to knit, perhaps, but mainly to learn Japanese. I think I'm going to struggle, because Japanese has a different writing system and the grammar's quite different, too, but I'm going to put my mind to it and I hope I can make some progress. (It's a good thing lots of signs are in the Latin alphabet, too, otherwise I'd be completely lost!) One of my friends told me to try to learn some Japanese before coming here – if only I'd listened to him! It'd be quite a bit easier now, I guess.

One of the truly wonderful things here is the food – you may remember that I've already raved about how much I love Japanese food. My favourite restaurant at home is Japanese, so I'm used to all of the dishes with seafood and rice, and I love them. But here – wow, the flavours are out of this world. Well, that's all for now. I'll write more soon!

9 **Read the blog again. What things does Jessica have to get used to?**

10 SPEAKING **Work in pairs. Think of two more possible things that Jessica might need to get used to. Compare your ideas.**

Changes

11 **Complete the sentences with words from the list.**

break | doing well | form | give up | ~~resolution~~ | struggle | taking up | ways

0 Jessica's made a ___*resolution*___ to use her travel time well.
1 She's thinking of ______________ knitting.
2 She thinks she's going to ______________ to learn Japanese.
3 She's started learning already, but so far she isn't ______________ .
4 Moving to another country is a chance to ______________ some new habits.
5 I love seafood, so I could never ______________ eating prawns.
6 I need to get fit, so I'll have to change my ______________ a bit.
7 I don't think I'm ever going to ______________ my bad habits.

Regrets: *I wish … / If only …*

12 **Complete the sentences from Jessica's blog. Then read again and check.**

1 I just wish someone ______________ me in advance about the number of people on the trains to and from school!
2 One of my friends told me to try to learn some Japanese before coming here – if only ______________ to him!

13 **Jessica wrote some emails to her friends back home. Complete the things she said. Use verbs from the list to help you.**

bring | find | know | ~~say~~ | wear

0 I didn't see Kylie before I left – I wish ___*I'd said*___ goodbye to her.
1 Electronic things here are really expensive – if only ______________ a little more money!
2 I went to a party last night and it was really hot – I wish ______________ a dress, not jeans.
3 There are lots of beautiful things to see here – if only ______________ a bit more about Japanese culture before we came.
4 Our flat here is quite small – I wish my dad ______________ a bigger one.

1 SURVIVAL INSTINCT

Get THINKING

Watch the video and think: are you adventurous?

OBJECTIVES

FUNCTIONS:
issuing and accepting a challenge

GRAMMAR:
verbs followed by infinitive or gerund; verbs which take gerund and infinitive with different meanings: *remember, forget, regret, try, stop*

VOCABULARY:
verbs of movement; adjectives to describe uncomfortable feelings

READING

1 **Look at the map and the photos. Which one shows *an outboard motor* and which one *a tarpaulin*? Which ocean can you see?**

2 SPEAKING **Imagine being in a small boat in the middle of the Pacific Ocean. What would you need to think about?**

3 **Read the article. Seven sentences have been removed from the article. Choose from the sentences A–H the one which fits each gap (1–7). There is one extra sentence.**

A The boys knew right away that they could only sit, wait and hope.
B Tears were shed again, but this time they were tears of joy and gratitude.
C A passing fishing boat spotted them and stopped to pick them up.
D The boat had no roof to protect them.
E All they could do was watch as it continued to sail away.
F But they would be proved wrong.
G Little did they know their journey would last over seven weeks.
H This meant they had something to drink.

4 1.01 **Read and listen to the article again and check your answers.**

5 SPEAKING **Work in pairs and discuss the statements.**

1 The boys should not have tried to make the trip without an adult.
2 If the boys had taken phones with them, they would have been found earlier.
3 I don't think I could survive a situation like that.
4 I would like to meet the three boys and ask them more about their experience.
5 How do you think you would deal with a situation like this? What would you find the most difficult?

Surviving for SEVEN WEEKS

Out in the Pacific Ocean, 500 km north of Samoa, lies a small group of islands called Tokelau. The population is only about 1400 people, but one day early in November 2010, 500 of them gathered for a memorial service for three teenagers. No one had seen 14-year-old Etueni Nasau, or his two 15-year-old cousins Samuel Pelesa and Filo Filo, for a month. Their boat was gone, too. When people realised that the three boys were missing, planes spent over three weeks trying to find them, but eventually they gave up. Their friends and relatives wept at their funeral service, believing that the boys were dead. [1] ____________________ .

In early October, the three boys had clambered into their small 3.5-metre boat because they felt like making a short trip to a neighbouring island. They had decided to take some coconuts and water with them, enough for a couple of days.

[2] ____________________ .

Not long after they headed out to sea, the boys lost sight of land and started to become disoriented. Then they ran out of fuel for their outboard motor, and started to drift. [3] ____________________ .

For days, they crouched in the boat under the fierce sun. Their water and coconuts quickly ran out. Sometimes, a small flying fish would fall into their boat and they would eat it, but this wasn't enough food for them. Once, a seabird landed on the boat – one of the boys leaped up and managed to grab it. They killed it and ate it, raw. At night there were often heavy rainstorms that threatened to overturn the boat, and the boys had to dive to the floor, holding on as hard as they could. But the storms also left a little rainwater in their canvas tarpaulin. [4] ____________________ .

They constantly kept watch for land or boats. One night, they saw the lights of a ship, but it was too far away to see them and they had no lights to attract attention. [5] ____________________ .

After several weeks, the night rains stopped. The boys were desperately thirsty, and, despite knowing the dangers of drinking seawater, they decided to sip some. Then, with perhaps only days, or even hours, to live, the thing they had been desperately hoping for, happened.

[6] ____________________ .

The boys were very weak but they managed to stagger onto the fishing boat. They began to recover after having some water and some food. From the boat, Filo Filo phoned his father, who rushed to pass on to the other villagers the scarcely believable news that the boys were safe and sound.

[7] ____________________ .

Train to THINK

Thinking rationally

Solving a problem requires decision-making. In a difficult situation we may need to make sure that we are not distracted by irrelevant ideas, so we can look at the facts that are relevant for making the right decision.

6 Which of these facts were relevant for the three boys in making their decision to drink some seawater?

1 They had no fresh water in the boat.
2 Seawater doesn't taste very nice.
3 Their boat was very small.
4 There were no clouds in the sky.
5 If you don't drink anything, you can die of dehydration.

7 SPEAKING Work in pairs and discuss how the boys may have felt when they made their decision.

8 SPEAKING Read the situations. For each one, think about what you might want to do and what you should do. Then compare your ideas with a partner.

1 You have an important test tomorrow and your friend wants you to go to a party tonight.
2 You haven't been feeling well for several days. A tells you to go to a doctor. B tells you to take some medicine. You like B better than A.
3 You borrowed a friend's bike and had a small accident – there's a scratch on the bike that isn't easy to see.

PRONUNCIATION
Diphthongs: alternative spellings Go to page 120.

GRAMMAR

Verbs followed by infinitive or gerund

1 Read the sentences from the article on page 13 and choose the correct words. There are two sentences in which both options are possible. Then complete the rules with *a gerund* and *an infinitive*.

1 They felt like *making / to make* a short trip to a neighbouring island.
2 One of the boys leaped up and managed *grabbing / to grab* it.
3 All they could do was watch as it continued *sailing / to sail* away.
4 They knew all the dangers of drinking seawater, but they decided *drinking / to drink* some.
5 A passing fishing boat spotted them and stopped *picking / to pick* them up.
6 They began *recovering / to recover*.

RULE: We follow the verbs:

- *imagine, feel like, suggest, practise, miss, can't stand, enjoy, detest* and *don't mind* with 7 ________________ .
- *manage, want, decide, refuse, hope, promise, ask, learn, expect, afford, offer* and *choose* with 8 ________________ .
- *begin, start* and *continue* with 9 ________________ or 10 ________________ with no difference in meaning.

2 Complete the sentences with the verbs in the list. Use the gerund or infinitive form.

buy | climb | get | go | help | read | show | walk

1 The weather was great on Sunday, but I didn't feel like ________________ a mountain.
2 My friend suggested ________________ on a bike ride.
3 Nobody asked us ________________ our tickets as we entered the cinema.
4 I gave Sienna a copy of Joe Simpson's book *Touching the Void*. She says she's really enjoying ________________ it.
5 Can I borrow your umbrella? I can't stand ________________ around in the rain.
6 I wanted ________________ new skis, but I couldn't afford them.
7 I don't mind ________________ my brother with his homework.
8 Can you imagine ________________ caught in a snowstorm for hours?

→ workbook page 10

VOCABULARY

Verbs of movement

3 Complete the sentences with the correct form of the verbs in the list. Then check your answers in the article on page 13.

dive | leap | rush | stagger

1 One of the boys ____________ up and managed to grab it.
2 The boys had to ____________ to the floor, holding on as hard as they could.
3 The boys were very weak but managed to ____________ onto the fishing boat.
4 He ____________ to give the incredible news to other villagers.

4 Match the words with the definitions.

1 climb | **2** crawl | **3** dive | **4** hop | **5** leap | **6** rush | **7** stagger | **8** swing | **9** tiptoe | **10** wander

a ☐ to jump on one foot
b ☐ to walk around without any clear purpose
c ☐ to move easily and without stopping in the air, backwards and forwards or from side to side
d ☐ to walk on your toes, especially in order not to make a noise
e ☐ to jump into water
f ☐ to go up, or to go towards the top of something
g ☐ to (cause to) go or do something very quickly
h ☐ to make a large jump from one place to another
i ☐ to move slowly on hands and knees
j ☐ to walk or move with difficulty as if you are going to fall

5 Complete the sentences with the correct forms of the verbs from Exercise 4.

1 He was really hot, so he ____________ into the swimming pool straightaway.
2 We spent the morning ____________ around the harbour, looking at the boats.
3 At the zoo, the monkeys were ____________ from the trees and ____________ to the top of them.
4 Their daughter was asleep, so they ____________ around the house.
5 Children learn to ____________ when they are babies, but they don't learn to ____________ on one foot until they are a bit older.
6 As soon as I heard Jo was back, I ____________ to her mum's house to see her.
7 With difficulty she managed ____________ to the phone to call for help.
8 He saw the snake, and in no time he ____________ onto the table.

→ workbook page 12

LISTENING

6 1.04 **Listen to a discussion on a radio show. What are the two people discussing?**

7 1.04 **Listen again. Mark the statements T (true) or F (false). Then correct the false statements.**

1 The man says that he didn't sleep very well during his exams. ☐
2 The woman says she didn't do enough serious revision. ☐
3 She says it's important to think about diet and sleep during an exam period. ☐
4 She says you should spend more time studying than enjoying yourself. ☐
5 She says you should not do more or less revision than your friends. ☐
6 The man was happy that he revised along with his friends. ☐
7 The woman thinks you should revise in whatever way is good for you. ☐
8 She thinks it's important to keep 100 percent to a schedule. ☐

8 SPEAKING **Work in pairs and do the following:**

1 List the pieces of advice the woman gives and say which ones you agree or disagree with.
2 Add one or two more pieces of advice for dealing with pre-exam stress.

GRAMMAR

Grammar video ▶02

Verbs which take gerund and infinitive with different meanings: *remember*, *forget*, *regret*, *try*, *stop*

9 **Complete the sentences from the listening with the verb in brackets. Use the correct form.**

1 Remember ______ regularly and well. (eat)
I still remember ______ sleepless nights. (have)
2 I really regret ______ it more seriously. (not take)
I regret ______ that we've run out of time. (say)
3 Try ______ comparing yourself with friends. (avoid)
I tried ______ together with friends. (revise)

RULE: *Remember, forget, regret*

Remember + [5] ______ means *thinking of a past experience you've had.*

Remember + [6] ______ means *don't forget to do something.*

Forget + [7] ______ means *to no longer think of something that you did.*

Forget + [8] ______ means *to not think of doing something you should do or should have done.*

Regret + [9] ______ means *feeling sorry about something you said or did in the past.*

Regret + [10] ______ means *feeling sorry about something you are going to say or do next or in the future.*

Other verbs

Try + [11] ______ means *try hard to see if you can do something that is really not easy.*

Try + [12] ______ means *do it and see what the results are.*

Stop + [13] ______ means *to not continue doing a certain activity or action.*

Stop + [14] ______ means *make a pause in one activity in order to do a different activity.*

10 **Match sentences 1–4 with pictures A–D. Then complete the rule with *gerund* or *infinitive*.**

1 She should stop to rest, but she needs to finish her work today.
2 She should stop resting, but she just doesn't want to go back to work.
3 He forgot to meet Sandra.
4 He'll never forget meeting Sandra for the first time.

11 **Complete each sentence with the correct form of the verbs in brackets.**

1 On the way to work, Dad stopped ______ some magazines. (buy)
2 I really regret ______ Jim. He's going to tell Martha, I'm sure. (tell)
3 When you go into town, please remember ______ some paper for the printer. (get)
4 Don't forget ______ food for my packed lunch tomorrow, Mum. (buy)
5 Sarah stopped ______ the guitar a few years ago. (play)
6 I just can't solve this puzzle. I've been trying ______ the answer for hours. (find)
7 My ankle hurts. I tried ______ some cream on it, but it hasn't helped. (put)
8 I remember ______ strawberry ice cream when I was very small. (love)

→ workbook page 11

VOCABULARY
Adjectives to describe uncomfortable feelings

1 Match the adjectives from the list with their definitions.

ashamed | awkward | desperate
guilty | puzzled | stuck

1 ____________________ : feeling extremely embarrassed about something you have done
2 ____________________ : feeling confused because you do not understand something
3 ____________________ : feeling you are in a difficult situation, or unable to change or get away from a situation
4 ____________________ : feeling embarrassed or uncomfortable
5 ____________________ : feeling worried or unhappy because you have done something wrong
6 ____________________ : feeling the need for or wanting something very much

2 Complete the sentences with the adjectives from Exercise 1.

1 When I'm with Mrs Meyer I always feel ____________________ . It's difficult to find something to talk about with her.
2 Ciara ought to be ____________________ of herself – talking to her mother like that!
3 Carl must have done something wrong, because he's looking so ____________________ .
4 After the earthquake, the people on the island were ____________________ for help.
5 We're a bit ____________________ as to why we haven't heard from them for weeks.
6 Without your help, we'd be ____________________ and wouldn't know what to do next.

→ workbook page 12

SPEAKING

3 When you have a problem and get stuck, which of these three things apply to you? Add three more of your own.

- ☐ I go online and look for some advice.
- ☐ I stop thinking about it and listen to some music.
- ☐ I start feeling helpless.

4 WRITING Write three sentences to describe problems and your emotional reactions to them. Use adjectives from Exercise 1.

I have a test tomorrow and I haven't studied enough. I'm desperate.
It was my best friend's birthday last Monday and I forgot to give her a present. I'm feeling guilty.

5 Work in small groups. Listen to each other's problems and tell each other what to do.

Stop feeling desperate. Maybe the test won't be very difficult. Otherwise, remember to start studying earlier next time.

Try to relax before the test. Listen to some music, or go for an early morning walk.

READING

6 Look at the photos and the headline of the article. Which of these things do you think are true about Miriam Lancewood?

- ☐ She is from New Zealand.
- ☐ She lives in a city.
- ☐ She sometimes hunts without a gun.
- ☐ She lives alone.
- ☐ She never eats meat.

7 1.05 Read and listen to the article to check your ideas.

8 Read the text again. Answer these questions based on your own opinions. Use evidence from the text to support your ideas.

1 How did Miriam feel about her life before 2010?
2 How does her husband feel about their lifestyle?
3 How happy is she about the way she leads her life?

How to SURVIVE in the WILDERNESS

Miriam Lancewood, from the Netherlands, has a university degree, but she has no permanent address and no job. She doesn't have a car, or a computer or a mobile phone. She doesn't have a bed, or a clock or a mirror. And she's very happy this way.

Miriam was living in New Zealand, in 2010, when she began to ask herself: could she survive a terrible natural disaster or a nuclear attack? Could she live without technology, electricity or other people? She decided that she didn't have the necessary skills or experience, so she and her husband Peter set off to live in the wilderness. They left their cottage, filled two 85-litre backpacks with some possessions and took 12 buckets of food to last the winter. And they've never looked back.

Since then, they have lived right in the middle of the wilderness of New Zealand's North Island. They live mostly in a tent or unequipped hut, with occasional returns to a town if their supplies are low – Lancewood sometimes plays guitar and sings on the street to earn a little money. Otherwise, they don't need anything from anyone.

In 2017, Miriam published a book – *Woman in the Wilderness* – which tells her story and recounts what she learned about nature, other people and herself. Life in the wilderness taught her how to manage with simple things, how to be alone, how to be bored, how to be afraid. She also talks about how she had to learn how to use a bow and arrow to hunt with, and the first time she killed a goat with one. Afterwards, she sat and cried because she had been brought up as a vegetarian. She and her husband ate the meat, because they did not want to waste a life and because it provided protein. Meat then became part of their diet.

Miriam and her husband Peter met in India. They spent two months in the Himalayas, trekking and meeting people who lived very simply in the mountains. The lifestyle attracted them both and once they were back in New Zealand, the idea of living in the wilderness became a possibility and eventually a reality. She does not for one moment regret choosing this way of life. 'If people don't agree with the way I live, well, it doesn't matter, does it?' she says.

WRITING
A diary page about an experience

9 Imagine you are Miriam Lancewood. Write a page of your diary. Write about:

- the activities you've been doing
- how you felt while you were doing them
- what you've learned from them.

Write 150–200 words.

WordWise: Expressions with *right*

10 Look at these sentences from the unit so far. Complete them with phrases from the list.

right | right away | right in the middle | rightly or wrongly

1 The boys knew ______________ that they could only sit, wait and hope.
2 Since 2010 they have lived ______________ of the wilderness.
3 ______________, the results of their exams will determine what they do next.
4 But you survived, ______________?

11 Complete the sentences with an expression with *right*.

1 You're the new girl at school, ______________?
2 Look at the time! We're late. We have to leave ______________.
3 There's going to be a new supermarket ______________ of town.
4 ______________, we have to switch off our phones before class starts.

→ workbook page 12

DEVELOPING SPEAKING

1 1.06 **Look at the photo. What do you think the two girls are doing? Read and listen to check.**

Ava: Sunday afternoon … I'm pretty bored.

Paloma: Same here. I think I'll just play some games on my phone.

Ava: Oh, phone, phone, phone. You know what, Paloma? You're addicted to that phone! You're always using it for something or other.

Paloma: Of course I'm not addicted to it. I could stop using it right now if I wanted to!

Ava: Really? OK, I challenge you, Paloma. I bet you can't survive three days without your phone.

Paloma: Seriously? Three days? That's too easy. You're on.

Ava: OK then. You'll have to give me your phone, though, and promise not to use anyone else's either.

Paloma: No problem.

Ava: You'll never manage to do this, Paloma, and you know it.

Paloma: Oh, I'll manage it, Ava, don't worry. And if I don't, we'll go to the burger place, you order whatever you want and I'll pay. Agreed?

Ava: It's a deal! I can't believe I'm … .

Paloma: Oh, just a moment Ava. A message from Mary. Give me two seconds … yes, replied. Sorry about that. Now, where were we?

Ava: We were talking about you not using your mobile – until you started using your mobile!

Paloma: Oh, you're right! I'm having second thoughts about this challenge. I think you're probably right. I can't do it!

Ava: I knew it! But we had a deal, so I still want my burger!

Paloma: Fair enough. Give me a shout when you know what day you want it.

2 1.06 **Read and listen to the dialogue again and answer the questions.**

1 What does Ava challenge Paloma to do?
2 What does Paloma promise to do if she loses?
3 How is their conversation interrupted?
4 Why does Paloma change her mind?

3 SPEAKING **Discuss the statements in pairs. Do you agree with them?**

1 It's possible to be addicted to your mobile phone.
2 Ava is being unfair when she challenges Paloma to not use her phone.

Phrases for fluency

4 **Find the underlined expressions in the dialogue and use them to complete the conversations.**

1 A I was really busy over the weekend. No time to relax! I always had [1]________________ to do.
B [2]________________ ! I didn't stop for a moment.

2 A Listen, if you find the homework difficult, [3]________________ and I can try to help you. Then maybe you can make us a snack later.
B [4]________________ ! Thanks a lot, Georgia.

3 A This exercise is exhausting.
B You're right [5]________________ ? We should have a break.

4 A Agreed. I think we should do that.
B Hang on, let me answer this phone call … Sorry about that. Right, [6]________________ ?

5 SPEAKING **Work in pairs. You are two friends who are bored and who are trying to find things to do. Try to use as many of the phrases from Exercise 4 as you can.**

FUNCTIONS
Issuing and accepting a challenge

KEY LANGUAGE

I bet you can't …	I think you're (probably) right.
Of course I can.	You'll never manage to …
I challenge you to …	No problem.
That's too easy.	I bet (you) I can …

6 **Read the phrases in the Key Language box. Which are used to issue a challenge? Which are used to accept or turn down a challenge?**

7 SPEAKING **Work in pairs. Write short dialogues, where one person challenges the other. Use these ideas or one of your own. Then act them out for the class.**

- eat a doughnut without licking your lips
- stay awake for 24 hours
- walk 20 kilometres in four hours
- finish this exercise before the pair next to us
- speak only in English during break times and lunchtimes for a whole week
- ________________________

LIFE COMPETENCIES

It can be important to try to do new things – it's by taking on challenges that we learn new skills and grow as people. But it's also important to be realistic about what you can achieve.

1 ▶ 03 **Watch the vlog. What challenge does Chloe set the audience? What challenge does she set herself?**

2 ▶ 03 **Watch the vlog again and make notes about:**

a the obstacles to the challenge
b the rewards of the challenge.

3 SPEAKING **Read the blog post. Work in pairs and answer the questions.**

1 Why did Sara decide to run a marathon?
2 Why was it a hard challenge for her?
3 What were the results of her running the marathon – for herself, and for others?
4 Was it a good idea for her to set herself this challenge? List positive and negative things.

4 **Imagine you are one of Sara's friends on the day that she told you she was going to run the London Marathon. What would you say to her?**

Me and my world

5 **Think of a time when you set yourself a challenge and make notes.**

- What was it?
- What did you do?
- What was the outcome?

6 SPEAKING **Work in pairs and tell your partner about your challenge.**

Last year, I started doing some volunteer work for a charity in my town that helps disabled children. I found out that the charity needed to buy some new wheelchairs, but that they really didn't have the money. So, I started to think about what I could do to raise money.

When I mentioned this to my friends, they said, 'Well, why don't you run the London Marathon?!' They laughed and so did I – we all know that I'm not an athlete at all. I've never done any running before. But later, I started to think that it might not be a bad idea.

I talked to the charity people and they agreed to put my name forward. I bought some gear and started running. I went out every night for a run and after a month or so, I found I could do almost five kilometres. The problem, though, is that the marathon is 42 kilometres!

The race was only five months away. I practised as hard as I could – I had to run and finish the race, because if I did, I would raise enough money from my sponsors to buy four new wheelchairs.

Well, when the big day came, I was not at all sure that I was ready. During my training, I'd managed to run 25 kilometres in one session, but 42? Could I do it? Fortunately, it wasn't a hot day and the people running with me helped me a lot. Nevertheless, after about 34 kilometres, I was exhausted and I nearly stopped, but the people watching cheered me on and I managed to struggle on to the finish line. My time was five hours and ten minutes. But I was in pretty bad shape and I was taken to hospital. I had to stay there overnight to recover, but they let me go home the next day.

It was hard, but I'm so proud that I did the marathon and got the wheelchairs for the charity.

TIPS FOR GIVING YOURSELF A CHALLENGE

- **When you set yourself a challenge, think about the possible outcomes – if you succeed, and if you don't succeed.**
- **Think about outcomes not only for yourself, but perhaps for other people, too.**
- **If you think it's a tough challenge, talk to other people you trust before making a decision about whether or not to accept the challenge.**

2 ON THE ROAD

OBJECTIVES

FUNCTIONS:
introducing information

GRAMMAR:
relative clauses (review); *which* to refer to a whole clause; omitting relative pronouns; reduced relative clauses

VOCABULARY:
groups of people; phrasal verbs (1)

Get THINKING

Watch the video and think: is there a lot of traffic congestion where you live?

A

C

B

D

READING

1 SPEAKING **Look at the people in the photos. Work in pairs and answer the questions.**

1 Where are these people going?
2 How are they feeling?
3 How are the people in the photos different from each other?

2 WRITING **Choose one of the people and write a short monologue about what they are thinking.**

3 **Look at the article and the photos on the next page. What do you think the article will be about?**

4 2.01 **Read and listen to the article to check your ideas.**

5 **Read the article again and answer the questions with the name of a person. Sometimes more than one name is possible.**

Who …
1 uses a hobby to get to work?
2 works in a school?
3 uses a talent that he learned when he was younger in his commute?
4 flies to get to work?
5 spends an hour and a half commuting each day?
6 gets wet on their way to work?
7 used to use public transport to get to work?
8 uses more than one type of transport to get to work?

6 SPEAKING **Work in pairs and discuss the questions.**

1 Which of these journeys sounds the most/least fun? Why?
2 What would be your perfect way to get to school?
3 What can be done to make people's commutes easier?

GETTING TO WORK

Most people's journey to work or school is usually quite simple – a short journey by car or on public transport. If you're very lucky, you might be able to walk or cycle. Of course, for some commuters it can be more tedious. Their workplace might not be so far from home, but heavy traffic can make it take much longer than it should. Their employer won't be happy if they're late. Suddenly, the commute becomes very stressful, which is not a great way to start the day.

However, there are some people who have found innovative ways to get to work.

Gabriel Horchler, who works in Washington DC, noticed that most of his commute took him alongside the river Anacostia. Being a keen rower, Gabriel realised that he didn't need to be sitting still in his car for hours, along with all the other motorists. So, he exchanged his car for a rowing boat and two bikes (one on each end). His journey, which now takes him 90 minutes, also helps him to keep fit.

Elsewhere in the US, Benjamin Keiffer beats the traffic by hopping on his unicycle and weaving his way through the New York traffic. It's a skill he learned as a boy at circus school. Benjamin says that it's the best part of his day and much better than when he used to travel on crowded subway trains or had to share the pavement with hundreds of other pedestrians who were all fighting for space.

But perhaps the most exciting commute of all belongs to Paul Cox. On holiday in Spain, Paul tried out paragliding and loved it. Now, when the weather allows him, he makes the 10-mile journey from his home in North Wales to work by paramotor!

However, there are some people who have to go to even greater lengths to get to work.

Abdul Mallik is a teacher in Malappuram, India. He teaches in a primary school which is only 7.5 miles from his home. It used to take him three hours to get there by bus, as his home and the school are separated by a river. But Abdul has found a unique way to get to work quicker – he walks through the river, even though the water is neck-high. Once on the other side, he changes into dry clothes and continues to the school.

This is nothing, however, compared to Elizabeth Miranda from the Philippines. Elizabeth is also a teacher, but her journey to join the rest of the staff at her school takes several hours and involves crossing five rivers. This means getting her feet and legs wet. It can be dangerous at times, but nothing will stop Elizabeth getting to school so that she can teach her students.

Train to THINK

Distinguishing fact from opinion

People often have disagreements because they confuse opinions with facts. A fact is something true for which there is usually proof. An opinion is a thought or belief and may not be true. When you want to know if what someone is saying is really true, it's important to ask the right questions to help you separate opinions from facts.

7 **Read the two statements (A). What is the purpose of the question (B) that follows each of them?**

1 A *Teenagers never want to travel anywhere with their parents.*
  B Does that mean that there has never been a young person who liked travelling with their parents?

2 A *I'm convinced listening to music keeps you healthy.*
  B What evidence is there that proves you are right?

8 SPEAKING **Here are things people said about their commute to work. Work in pairs and think of good questions that you could ask to separate opinions from facts.**

1 I spend half my life in my car.
2 The government needs to spend a lot more money on public transport.
3 Commuting is bad for your mental health.
4 People would be healthier if they could work from home.
5 People are too selfish to use public transport.

GRAMMAR
Relative clauses (review)

1 **Read the sentences from the article on page 21. Look at the underlined parts. Then complete the rule by writing A, B, C or D.**

A His journey, which now takes him 90 minutes, also helps him to keep fit.

B He teaches in a primary school which is only 7.5 miles from his home.

C He had to share the pavement with other pedestrians who were all fighting for space.

D Gabriel Horchler, who works in Washington DC, noticed that ...

> **RULE:** We use a defining relative clause to identify an object (*which/that*), a person (*who/that*), a place (*where*) or a possession (*whose*). Without this information, it's hard to know who or what we're talking about (e.g. sentences [1]___ and [2]___).
> We use a non-defining relative clause to add extra information. We don't need this information to understand the sentence. We put commas around it (e.g. sentences [3]___ and [4]___).

2 SPEAKING **Complete each sentence with *who*, *which* or *that*. Are they defining or non-defining relative clauses? Then discuss the statements in pairs.**

1 I don't understand people ____________ decide to drive to work instead of walking.
2 I don't like people ____________ eat their lunch next to me on a bus.
3 A commuter is just someone ____________ is trying to get to work.
4 It's buses being dirty ____________ make me not want to use them.

3 **Join the sentences to make one sentence with a non-defining relative clause. Put commas in the correct places.**

0 The workers were tired. They had travelled a long way to work.
The workers, who had travelled a long way, were tired.
1 The motorist was driving too fast. The motorist shouted at me.
2 London is a busy city. It is where I work.
3 I've been reading a book by William Boyd on my commute. Boyd is one of my favourite writers.
4 Juan has been working here for ten years. He is from Spain.

which to refer to a whole clause

4 **Read the sentence from the article on page 21. What does *which* refer to?**

Suddenly, the commute becomes very stressful, which is not a great way to start the day.

5 **What does *this* refer to in these sentences? Rewrite them as one sentence.**

0 A lot of commuters use their car. This is bad for the environment.
A lot of commuters use their car, which is bad for the environment.
1 Some people at my office commute for over an hour. This is tiring.
2 I have to be at work by 8 o'clock. This can be difficult.
3 My boss doesn't mind if I'm late sometimes. This makes life easier.
4 People can get very stressed in heavy traffic. This often leads to arguments.

→ workbook page 18

VOCABULARY
Groups of people

6 **Complete each sentence with a word from the list.**

~~commuters~~ | employees | employers | immigrants | inhabitants | motorists | pedestrians | politicians | refugees | residents | the crew | the staff

0 People who travel to work are *commuters* .
1 People who walk on a street or pavement are called ____________ .
2 A group of people who work for an organisation are ____________ .
3 People who drive cars are called ____________ .
4 A group of people who work on a plane or ship are ____________ .
5 ____________ are people or animals that live in a specific place.
6 People who are paid to work for other people are called ____________ .
7 People who work in politics are called ____________ .
8 ____________ are people who have to leave their own country because it's too dangerous to live there.
9 ____________ pay others to work for them.
10 People who live in a certain place are the ____________ .
11 ____________ are people who go to a different country to live there permanently.

→ workbook page 20

LISTENING

7 SPEAKING **Work in pairs. Look at the photos and the maps. Which animals in the photos make which journeys on the maps?**

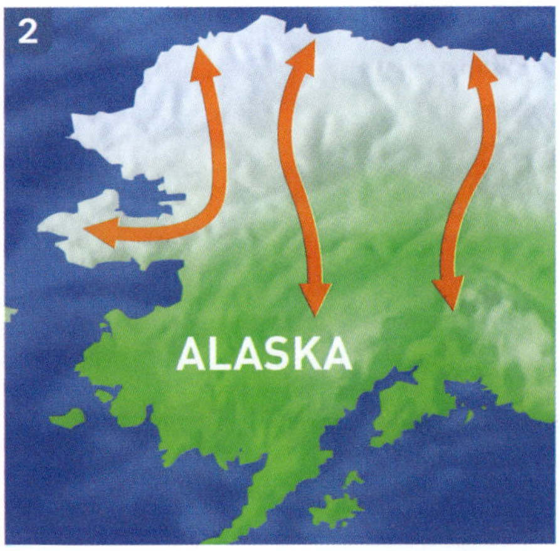

8 2.02 **Listen to the radio quiz to check your ideas. Write 1–3 in the boxes.**

9 2.02 **Listen again and choose the correct answer, A, B or C.**

1 What is this quiz round about?
  A animal migration
  B famous animals
  C animals in nature
2 What's the most amazing fact about the bar-tailed godwit's migration?
  A It's the longest migration of any bird.
  B It does it in a day.
  C It does it without stopping.
3 How many times in their life do freshwater eels find themselves in the Sargasso Sea?
  A one
  B two
  C three
4 What makes the caribou's journey more difficult?
  A They make it on foot.
  B They have to do it through heavy snows.
  C They make it four times a year.

10 SPEAKING **Work in pairs and discuss the questions.**

1 Which of these animals do you think is the most amazing and why?
2 What animals migrate to and from your country?

FUNCTIONS

Introducing (amazing) information

11 2.02 **Listen again to the radio quiz. Complete the phrases used to introduce information with the missing words.**

1 Believe it or ______________ …
2 Did you ______________ that …?
3 Would you ______________ me if I told you …?
4 What's most ______________ about … is …

12 SPEAKING **Work in pairs. Person A thinks of something amazing that he/she knows. (Invent something if you want!) Person A gives the information to person B, using one of the expressions in Exercise 11. Then A and B change roles.**

A BRAZILIAN ADVENTURE

Last year, after I finished school, I realised I didn't really have a plan for the next stage of my life. My mum, who is Brazilian but has lived here in the UK most of her life, had the great idea of sending me over to Brazil to live with one of her aunts for a while. At first, I wasn't sure, but after two months of sitting around the house doing nothing, I began to think an overseas adventure sounded like a pretty good idea! And if nothing else, it meant I wouldn't have to put up with my annoying baby sister for a year. (Just kidding, Nina!)

So, I started doing the things I needed to do to bring it about – a few phone calls, a visit to the Brazilian embassy and shopping for more summer clothes! Two weeks later, I was at the airport setting out for Rio de Janeiro. Thirteen hours later, the plane touched down. I had arrived. I was worn out but really, really excited.

I've been here half a year now. My aunt and my cousins have made me feel wonderfully at home. I've even got a job. I'm teaching English to children living in some of the poorer parts of the city.

I think the best thing about it so far has been learning about another culture. At school I had several friends whose families came from different parts of the world originally. I think I had quite a good understanding of some other cultures, but actually living in another country means you really get to see how life there can be different and similar to the one you know. I've been through so many different experiences here, and mostly they've been brilliant. I feel like I've learned a lot more about the world and also about myself. I'm a lot more independent than I ever thought I could be! I've made loads of friends and I run into several people each time I leave the house. It really makes me feel like I'm at home here.

It's also been brilliant to learn another language. My mum never spoke Portuguese at home, which was a shame. Of course, I heard it spoken a lot whenever my relatives visited and I knew a few words, but I was amazed at how quickly I've managed to pick it up. After a few months of hanging out with my cousin and her friends, I'm finding I understand most of what they say and I'm able to take part in their conversations quite easily. It's great finally having a second language and learning it doesn't seem like work at all. I've also become really interested in photography. There are so many beautiful views to take photos of!

My year abroad is turning out to be the best year of my life so far. And who knows, I might be here longer, much longer!

READING

1 Look at the photos and the title of the blog. Work in pairs and discuss the questions.

1 Where do you think Sam is?
2 Where do you think he's from?
3 What is the article about?

2 2.03 **Read and listen to the blog to check your ideas.**

3 Read the blog again and answer the questions.

1 What is Sam's connection to Brazil?
2 Why did he decide to spend a year in Brazil?
3 What is he doing in Brazil?
4 What has he learned from his experiences so far?
5 Why does he feel at home in Brazil?
6 How is he getting on with the language?

VOCABULARY
Phrasal verbs (1)

4 Complete these sentences from the blog. Use the correct form of the phrasal verbs from the list. Then read the blog again to check.

bring about | go through | pick up | put up with | set out for | touch down | turn out | wear out

1 So I started doing the things I needed to do to ________ it ________ .
2 I was ________ ________ , but really, really excited.
3 I've ________ ________ so many different experiences here.
4 Thirteen hours later, the plane ________ ________ .
5 I wouldn't have to ________ ________ ________ my annoying baby sister for a year.
6 I was amazed at how quickly I've managed to ________ it ________ .
7 Two weeks later, I was at the airport ________ ________ ________ Rio de Janeiro.
8 My year abroad is ________ ________ to be the best year of my life.

PRONUNCIATION
Phrasal verb stress Go to page 120.

5 Match the phrasal verbs from Exercise 4 with their meanings.

0 make (someone) very tired *wear out*
1 start a journey ______
2 learn (informally) ______
3 tolerate ______
4 experience (a difficult situation) ______
5 have a particular result ______
6 land ______
7 make happen ______

6 SPEAKING Work in pairs and discuss the questions.

1 How do you feel when you set out on holiday?
2 What wears you out?
3 Can you think of any habits someone you know has that you have to put up with?
4 What difficulties does someone have to go through when they leave school and start university?
5 Do you think it's possible to pick up new words from listening to English-language songs?

→ workbook page 20

GRAMMAR

Grammar video ▶05

Omitting relative pronouns

7 Read the two sentences from the blog. Where can you put *that* in each sentence? Is *that* the subject or object of the relative clause? Complete the rule with the words *subject* and *object*.

1 I started doing the things I needed to do.
2 I run into several people I know each time I leave the house.

RULE: When the relative pronouns *that / which / who* are the [3] ______ of a defining relative clause, they can be omitted. But if they are the [4] ______ of the defining relative clause, they can't be omitted.

8 Read these sentences. Put a tick (✓) if you can omit the pronoun in *italics*, or a cross (✗) if you can't.

1 You'll miss the friends *who* you used to hang out with. ☐
2 I ran into some people *who* couldn't wait to leave. ☐
3 I've decided to write about some of the challenges *that* living abroad can bring. ☐
4 You become one of those people *who* wish they'd stayed at home. ☐
5 There's new vocabulary *which* you have to pick up. ☐
6 There's no country in the world *that* suits everybody. ☐

→ workbook page 19

Reduced relative clauses

9 Read these sentences. Where can you put *that was* and *who are*? Tick (✓) the correct box in the rule.

1 I'm teaching English to children living in some of the poorer parts of the city.
2 I was boarding a plane heading for Rio de Janeiro.

RULE: When relative clauses begin with a relative pronoun + the auxiliary verb *be*, we can omit:
A ☐ only the relative pronoun
B ☐ the relative pronoun + the verb *be*.

10 Cross out the words/phrases in *italics* that can be omitted.

Footballers [1]*who* come from other countries to play in the UK often have problems adjusting to their new lives. Some of the players [2]*who are* playing in the UK are quite young, so they easily feel homesick. And then there are things like food – people [3]*who were* brought up on spicy food or exotic fruit don't always like typical British food. But the biggest problems [4]*that* they face seem to be the weather and the language. The country [5]*that* they come from might be very hot, which the UK isn't. It isn't always easy for players [6]*who* come from Brazil or Mexico, for example, to adapt to the grey skies and short winter days [7]*that* they experience in England. And not all the foreign players find it easy to learn English – the ones [8]*who* do, tend to find it easier to adapt.

TH!NK values

Learning from other cultures

11 Imagine you live in another country. What three things would you find most difficult/enjoy most about it?

12 Choose the options that are true for you. Make notes about your reasons.

1 *I'd like / I wouldn't like* to visit other countries.
2 *I'd like / I wouldn't like* to live in another country.
3 *I'm interested / I'm not interested* in other cultures.
4 Knowing about other cultures *helps / doesn't help* me understand my own culture.
5 *I think / I don't think* it's good to have people from other countries living in my country.

13 SPEAKING Compare your ideas about Exercises 11 and 12 with the class. How similar or different are you to your classmates?

TH!NK

Nomadic people and animals

Culture

NOMADIC PEOPLE

1 SPEAKING Work in pairs and look at the photos and the title. Where do you think the groups of people live?

2 2.06 Read and listen to the text to check your ideas.

Most of us are used to living in the same place – every day, all year round, we go 'home'. But for some people around the world, home is a place that moves, often across international borders. Here are three groups of people who have or had a nomadic way of life.

1 THE TLINGIT

The Tlingit are found on the islands and the shores between Canada and Alaska. They were once a much larger group of people, but the arrival of Europeans in the 1770s brought the Tlingit into contact with diseases, such as smallpox, against which they had no immunity. Many of them died.

They have their own language, in which their name translates as 'people from the tides'. Unsurprisingly, the sea has played a huge role in their lives, particularly as a source of food. Their diet consists of a lot of fish, seal meat and seaweed. They also hunt deer, bears and goats, and collect berries and other plants from the forests.

Today, around 15,000 Tlingit still live in the area, and although most of them have a much more modern way of life, some are still trying to live off the land in the way that their ancestors did.

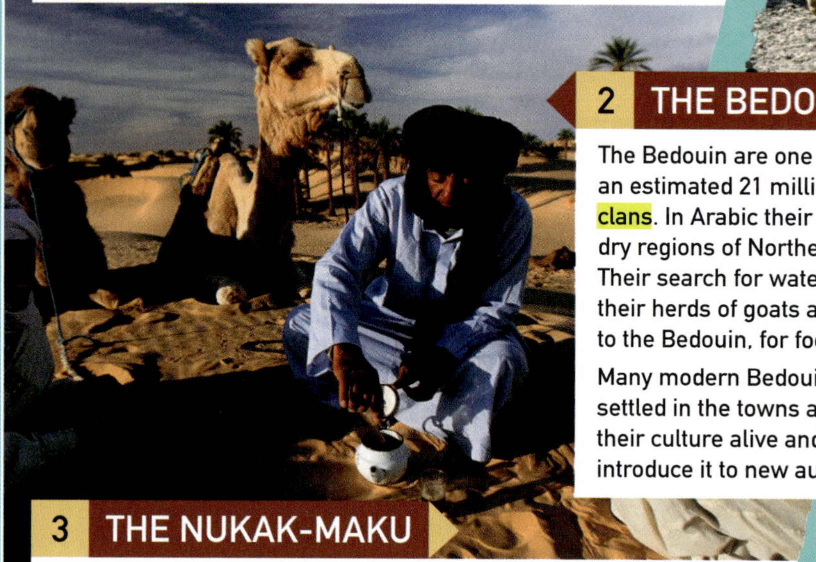

2 THE BEDOUIN

The Bedouin are one of the most well-known nomadic tribes and there are an estimated 21 million Bedouin in the world today, split into many different clans. In Arabic their name means 'desert dwellers', as they have lived in the dry regions of Northern Africa and the Arabian peninsula for over 1,000 years. Their search for water sources means they are always on the move, taking their herds of goats and camels with them. These two animals are essential to the Bedouin, for food, dairy products and for trading with other clans.

Many modern Bedouin have left their nomadic lifestyle behind them and have settled in the towns and cities of the region. However, they are keen to keep their culture alive and organise annual festivals to celebrate their heritage and introduce it to new audiences.

3 THE NUKAK-MAKU

The Nukak-Maku are a nomadic tribe that lives deep inside the Amazon rainforest in Colombia. For hundreds of years, they lived unknown to the outside world. They were only discovered in 1981. Unfortunately, contact with civilisation meant they were exposed to new illnesses and many died from these diseases. Their land is also under threat from people wanting to grow coca trees. These days, fewer than 1,000 Nukak-Maku are thought to remain there and they are at risk of becoming extinct.

They live in very small groups and are always on the move, staying in one place for only a few days before moving on to their next destination. They are true masters of survival and use poisoned darts and blow pipes to hunt jungle animals such as monkeys, birds and wild pigs.

3 Read the article again and answer the questions.

According to the article, which group (or groups):

1 relies heavily on the sea?
2 has only recently become known to the world?
3 has seen many of their people move to towns?
4 lives in an area where water is difficult to find?
5 is in danger of not surviving?
6 has modernised the way they live?

4 VOCABULARY Match the highlighted words in the article with the definitions.

1 the places where one country ends and another begins
2 on a journey or trip, the place you want to get to
3 all the things that you eat
4 defence against a disease
5 small groups of people
6 having died out completely
7 happening once every year
8 stay

5 SPEAKING Work in pairs and discuss the questions.

1 Do you know of any other groups of people who are nomadic? What do you know about their culture?
2 What do you think might be the advantages and disadvantages of a nomadic lifestyle?
3 The article says that the Nukak-Maku may become extinct. What do you think could be done to protect these people?

WRITING
An informal email

1 INPUT Read Giulia's email and answer the questions.

1 How long has she been with the Inuit people?
2 When did she try to catch a seal?
3 What does she say strikes her most about the Inuit?

2 ANALYSE Match words or phrases from the email with these meanings.

1 a great deal
2 I have finally arrived
3 agreed that I could accompany them
4 I am extremely happy
5 my experiences here
6 one or two days ago

3 Why does Giulia not use the phrases in Exercise 2 in her email?

4 PLAN Imagine you are spending two weeks living with one of the nomadic tribes mentioned in the article on page 26, and make notes.

- Choose which of the three groups you are living with.
- Decide what things in general have been good/ not so good about your experiences so far.
- Decide on one specific thing about their life that has really impressed you.

5 PRODUCE Write an email to an English-speaking friend (about 200 words).

- Make sure to start and end your email appropriately.
- Talk generally about your experiences first, then move on to more specific details.
- Check your writing to make sure that your language is not too formal.

Giulia
Giulia@thinkmail.com

Hi James,

How are you doing? Hope you're OK!

Well, here I am at last – living in northern Canada with the nomadic Inuit people. You know that I've been wanting to do this for years and my dream has finally come true. I'm over the moon to be here.

I got here ten days ago and I'm staying with a family who said I could go along with them to hunt. I've already done some amazing things – sleeping in an igloo, for example, and watching the Inuit people go hunting for fish and for small animals.

The most difficult thing to deal with, of course, is the cold. There's also the fact that you have to keep moving every few days to find food. The way they hunt is interesting. The Inuit make a hole in the ice and hope that a seal will appear so that they can catch it. I went hunting with my host dad a couple of days ago – he showed me how to make a hole and then we stood for six hours in the freezing cold, waiting for a seal to appear. It never came. I got so fed up. But then I thought, 'Hey, the Inuit people do this every day, sometimes waiting for ten hours. And sometimes they catch a seal and sometimes they don't. What's my problem?' What amazes me most about them is their patience and my own is getting loads better!

Well, I'll write and tell you more about how I'm getting on with things when I can. Hope you're well!

All the best,
Giulia

B2 First for Schools

READING AND USE OF ENGLISH

Part 4: Key word transformations

→ workbook page 117

1 For questions 1–6, complete the second sentence so that it has a similar meaning to the first sentence, using the word given. Do not change the word given. You must use between two and five words, including the word given. Here is an example (0).

0 I think taking the 8 pm train is the best idea.
PREFER
I'd *prefer to take* the 8 pm train.

1 I've been studying all day and I'm really tired.
ME
Studying all day ______________ out.

2 I wish I hadn't gone to bed so late.
REGRET
I ______________ to bed so late.

3 I got really annoyed by Paul and Dave laughing all the time.
WHICH
Paul and Dave kept laughing, ______________ me.

4 That kind of behaviour should not be tolerated by anyone.
PUT
No-one ______________ that kind of behaviour.

5 Please make sure you lock the door.
FORGET
Please ______________ the door.

6 Getting up early in the morning is the worst thing.
STAND
I ______________ up early in the morning.

Part 1: Multiple-choice cloze

→ workbook page 97

2 For questions 1–8, read the text below and decide which answer (A, B, C or D) best fits each gap. There is an example at the beginning (0).

The Great Migration of wildebeest in Africa is [0] C the world's most impressive wildlife [1]___. Every year, around two million of these strange animals [2]___ a huge, circular journey of 3,000 kilometres or so, [3]___ grass and water. The exact [4]___ they follow depends very much on the seasons and where there is rainfall. At one point on their journey, the animals get to the Grumeti and Mara rivers and they need to [5]___ the fast-flowing and crocodile-infested waters in order to [6]___. Usually, they are very hesitant to go in, and can wait for hours or days at the river bank, but [7]___, one wildebeest jumps into the water and all the others follow. Thousands are taken by the crocodiles, but the survivors have the [8]___ of fresh grass on the other side. They won't have to face the crocodiles for another year!

	A	B	C	D
0	at	in	(among)	around
1	views	glimpses	incidents	spectacles
2	make	do	have	participate
3	searching	seeking	looking	viewing
4	way	direction	map	route
5	overtake	walk	cross	leave
6	proceed	run on	prolong	carry out
7	ultimately	eventually	lastly	lately
8	review	release	reward	reassurance

WRITING

Part 1: An essay

→ workbook page 43

3 Write your answer in 140–190 words in an appropriate style.

In your English class, you have been talking about inventions. Now your English teacher has asked you to write an essay for homework. Write your essay using **all** the notes and giving reasons for your point of view.

Technological or scientific inventions are responsible for some of the biggest changes we can see in the world today. What do you think?

Notes

Write about:

1 transport
2 communication
3 ______________ (your own idea)

TEST YOURSELF UNITS 1 & 2

VOCABULARY

1 Complete the sentences with the words in the list. There are four extra words.

crawl | go through | guilty | motorists | puzzled | ran into | refugees
residents | rushing | staff | stuck | turned out | wandering | worn out

1 Sally was ______________________ slowly around the shop looking for a present for her mum's birthday.
2 I hadn't seen Marie for ages, but yesterday I ______________________ her at the cinema.
3 I saw a documentary about ______________________ fleeing across borders to escape the war.
4 I'm so happy that I passed my driving test. It was awful and I wouldn't want to ______________________ that again!
5 You haven't done anything wrong – you don't have to feel ______________________ about anything, OK?
6 Mr Sawyer runs a small business. He has a ______________________ of four people.
7 They are all local ______________________. Most of them live in the streets near us.
8 My little sister can't walk yet, but she can ______________________ really fast!
9 I was ______________________ by my friend's reaction – I couldn't understand why she laughed.
10 The beginning of the film was very sad, but it all ______________________ okay in the end.

/10

GRAMMAR

2 Complete the sentences. Use the verbs in the list, with *to* + infinitive, or with a gerund (*-ing* form). Use two of the verbs twice.

do | fall | go | live

1 Yesterday my friends decided ______________________ to the beach to play volleyball.
2 My brother says he remembers ______________________ out of bed when he was two years old.
3 Jack always forgets ______________________ his homework and then gets in trouble.
4 I want ______________________ in Paris one day.
5 I don't mind ______________________ the washing up at home.
6 I hate being in an empty house. I can't imagine ______________________ alone.

3 Find and correct the mistake in each sentence.

1 I really like that guy which plays Sam on TV.
2 My brother Julian that lives in New York is coming to stay with me.
3 It isn't a film makes everyone laugh.
4 The man what plays the drums in the band is on the left in the photo.
5 My brother broke my phone, what means he has to buy me a new one.
6 She's the runner won the gold medal.

/12

FUNCTIONAL LANGUAGE

4 Choose the correct options.

1 A Next week Rebecca's going to run a 15-kilometre race. That's *quite a* / *really* distance.
B Yes, it is. And she only started running a couple of months ago, too. That's *amazing* / *daring*.
2 A I heard that you got 95%. That's *OK* / *phenomenal*. Well done!
B Thanks. I could hardly believe it. And my parents thought it was *incredible* / *quite*.
3 A I'*m betting* / *bet* you can't say 'Good morning' in five different languages.
B Well, you're right – of course I *can* / *can't*.
4 A You *can* / *will* never manage to stay off the internet for two days.
B Mm, I think you're right, but I *dare* / *can dare* you to stop using Whatsapp for a week!

/8

MY SCORE /30

22–30 | 10–21 | 0–9

3 GROWING UP

OBJECTIVES

FUNCTIONS:
emphasising

GRAMMAR:
quantifiers; *so* and *such* (review); *do* and *did* for emphasis

VOCABULARY:
costumes and uniforms; bringing up children

Get THINKING

Watch the video and think:
what's the hardest part of being a teenager?

A

C

B

D

READING

1 SPEAKING **Look at the photos and discuss the questions in pairs.**

1 Do you enjoy dressing up? Why do you think people enjoy wearing costumes?
2 Do you think fancy dress is just for kids?
3 Do you think it's okay to make animals wear costumes? Why (not)?

2 SPEAKING **Look again at the photos, and look at the title and the photo on the next page. What do you think the blog will be about?**

3 3.01 **Read and listen to the blog to check your ideas.**

4 **Read the blog again and answer the questions.**

1 What did Rain's parents do on his first day of high school?
2 How many days did Rain's dad, Dale, wave at the bus?
3 Which other family members got involved?
4 What were the first and last costumes that Dale wore?
5 How much did Dale spend on the costumes?
6 How did he keep the cost so low?
7 What did Rain think about his dad dressing up at the beginning? And at the end?
8 What happened at the beginning of the next school year?

5 SPEAKING **Work in pairs and discuss the questions.**

1 Does Dale sound like a good dad? Explain your reasons.
2 How would you feel if your dad was like Dale? Why?
3 Why do you think Dale wanted to dress up?

AN EMBARRASSING DAD

If you think you have the world's most embarrassing dad, then think again.

American teenager Rain Price was waved off to school from the bus stop outside his house, by his dad, every day for a whole school year. OK, so that doesn't sound too bad, but this was no ordinary goodbye, because each day Rain's dad did it while wearing a different fancy-dress costume!

It all started on 16-year-old Rain's first day of high school. Like many proud parents, Rochelle and Dale, Rain's mum and dad, sent him off to school with a big wave from the doorstep. That evening Rain made the mistake of complaining about how embarrassing they were, which gave Dale a great idea.

The next morning, as Rain stepped onto the bus outside his house, he could hear all of his school friends laughing at something. He turned around and to his horror, there was his dad waving him off, dressed as an American football player, complete with ball and helmet. But that was just the beginning. For the next 180 school days, come rain or shine, Dale waved goodbye to his son dressed in a different costume. One day he was a king waving his sword and shield, the next a chef in his hat and apron, the following a pirate. Then there was Elvis and Wonder Woman.

Dale even got other members of the family involved, using Rain's younger brother to play Batman alongside his Robin.

Amazingly, Dale only spent $50 on all of the costumes. He got loads of costumes from the family fancy-dress collection and then there were several friends and neighbours who were happy to help.

Some of Rain's friends didn't find it funny, but most of them looked forward to seeing what Dale would be wearing every day. And Dale found an international audience for his dressing up, too, as each day Rochelle took a photo of her husband in fancy dress and put it on their blog, waveatthebus.blogspot.com, which became a hit on the internet. Even Rain was eventually able to see the funny side and realised that his dad was pretty cool after all.

For the final farewell on the last day of school, Dale dressed up as a pirate and stood next to a sign which said: 'It's been fun waving at the bus. Have a great summer.' But all good things don't always come to an end. The new school year began, and Dale was there again, in fancy dress, to wave at the bus.

Train to TH!NK

Changing your opinions

It can be a mistake to believe something just because it's based on an opinion you've formed. Becoming a critical thinker means continually reflecting on your opinions, and being willing to change them if they aren't based on evidence.

6 Which people from the story may have had these opinions at some point? Write their names.

1 'My dad is the most embarrassing person in the world.' ____________________

2 'Rain's dad is really silly.' ____________________

3 'I don't think Dale should do this – it's going to cost a lot of money.' ____________________

7 SPEAKING Work in pairs and discuss how the people's opinions in Exercise 6 changed throughout the school year and why.

Initially, Rain thought that his dad was the most embarrassing dad in the world. But, with time, he realised that maybe that wasn't true. He learned to appreciate his dad's sense of humour.

8 SPEAKING Work in groups and discuss some opinions that you or family members have had that have changed. Think about music, school, fashion, friends, etc.

GRAMMAR
Quantifiers

Grammar video ▶08

1 **Look at the blog on page 31 and complete the sentences. Then complete the rule with *loads of, a little, all, several* and *none*.**

1 Like ____________________ proud parents …
2 He could hear ____________________ of his school friends laughing at something.
3 He got ____________________ of costumes from the family fancy-dress collection.
4 There were ____________________ friends and neighbours happy to help.
5 ____________________ of his friends didn't find it funny, but ____________________ of them looked forward to it.

> **RULE:** Quantifiers are words and expressions that we use to talk about amount.
>
> 0%
> [6] ____________________
> *hardly any*
> *a few /* [7] ____________________,
> *not many / much, a small number of*
> *some /* [8] ____________________
> [9] ____________________ */ a lot of, lots of, plenty, much / many, a good deal of*
> *most, almost all, the vast majority of*
> [10] ____________________
> 100%

2 **Choose the correct words.**

1 I've got *a few / loads of* followers on my YouTube channel – more than 20,000.
2 I spend *a lot of / hardly any* time with my friends – we meet up every day after school and most weekends, too.
3 I spend *most / hardly any* of my time on my tablet. It's the most important thing I've got.
4 *A small number / Most* of my teachers are really nice. I really like this school.
5 *Most / All* of my family live near me, but I've got an uncle who lives in Australia.
6 I spend *almost all / hardly any* of my money on downloads. I don't really care about music.

3 SPEAKING **Work in pairs and discuss the sentences in Exercise 2. Which of them are true for you?**

→ workbook page 28

VOCABULARY
Costumes and uniforms

4 SPEAKING **Look at the list of clothes and accessories. What costumes might people use these items for? Discuss in pairs.**

- sword and shield
- leather jacket
- wig
- snorkel
- poncho
- helmet
- bathrobe
- mask
- apron
- football top

5 **Look at the photos. Who is wearing a costume? Who is wearing a uniform? Who is wearing a kit?**

A

B

C

6 SPEAKING **Work in pairs and discuss the questions.**

1 Do you or does anybody you know wear a uniform for work? Describe it.
2 Can you list five jobs in which people wear uniforms?
3 Describe a sports kit to your partner, but don't say what sport it's for. Can your partner guess?
4 Describe your perfect costume to wear to a fancy-dress party.

→ workbook page 30

LISTENING

7 Look at the photos. What do you think the podcast will be about?

8 3.02 Listen to the podcast. Mark the sentences T (true) or F (false).

1 This is a story with a tragic ending. ☐
2 This is a heart-warming story of a father's love for his daughter. ☐
3 We learn how a father is motivated by his daughter's love of the outdoors. ☐
4 Ricky van Beek regularly competes in the Paralympics with his daughter, Maddy. ☐
5 Many people are inspired by watching the father and daughter duo compete in triathlons. ☐

9 3.02 Listen again and choose the correct answers.

1 What is unusual about Maddy and her father, Ricky van Beek, competing together in outdoor races?
A Ricky finds walking difficult.
B Maddy has a condition that means she is unable to walk.
C Maddy has a fear of water.

2 What was a major handicap for Ricky when they began racing?
A He smoked heavily and he was not very fit.
B He couldn't give up smoking.
C He didn't like running on bumpy roads.

3 What is the main motivation for Ricky?
A the feeling of freedom that running gives him
B seeing the joy that it gives his daughter
C being an inspiration to others

4 What will Ricky do if Maddy can no longer race with him?
A He will give up racing.
B He will continue to race with her in his heart.
C He will find another sport for her to participate in.

5 How does seeing them race together make people feel?
A They are inspired to take part in future marathons.
B They wish that they could race with their daughters.
C They feel moved by the love Ricky's actions show for his daughter.

SPEAKING

10 Work in pairs and discuss the questions.

Look at the examples below. Have your parents or your siblings ever made a similar sacrifice for you or a good cause you are passionate about?

- done a sponsored swim or walk with you
- baked cakes to help you raise money for charity
- climbed a mountain with you
- helped you when you were scared
- given up their time to teach you to play a musical instrument

11 Have you ever done any of these things, or something similar, for a brother or sister, or a friend?

TO SHARENT OR NOT TO SHARENT

'I can't believe you put that photo of me on Instagram!'

Does this sound familiar? Do your parents post photos of you online? Are there photos out there that you really don't want the world to see?

We all know that parents just want to do their best for their children. However, parents around the world are creating a digital footprint for their children before they can give consent. Future employers might be able to access those images online.

French police have warned that parents could face future lawsuits from their children for violating their privacy. Under French privacy law, you are currently not allowed to publish a photo of someone without their consent.

Some children have publicly asked their parents not to share photos on Instagram or on their blogs. Children grow up fast and parents must respect that.

'Mom, we've discussed this. You may not post anything without my consent.' Apple Martin famously wrote the above comment under a selfie taken by her famous mother, Gwyneth Paltrow, of the two of them skiing, and a media storm followed.

The daughter of Christie Tate, a mummy blogger, found lots of essays and photos of herself online when she googled herself. She did ask her mother if the content could be taken down, but her mother refused.

Ray Fitzgerald, a parenting coach, advises his followers to stick to the 'three P rules of posting':

- **PRIVACY** – Make sure private images stay private and check that your privacy settings are as tight as possible.
- **PERCEPTION** – If you were a teenager, would you like your parents to share that picture of you online? If the answer is no, then don't post it.
- **PERMISSION** – Always ask a teenager's permission before posting an image.

I asked some teenagers and here are some of their comments:

> 'I don't usually mind. My mum and dad have given me a very happy childhood. They've been great parents. But then last week my mum shared a picture of me and her in the park. It was such a bad picture. I was so embarrassed. Sharenting is bad news.' **SAM**

> 'My mum has so few followers, I don't mind. But it's different if your parents are famous or have thousands of followers. Gwyneth Paltrow is very famous and so many people saw that skiing picture. I do think her daughter was right to be angry.' **JACK**

> 'I did see the picture and I do follow Gwyneth Paltrow. I didn't think the picture itself was so terrible. However, I do understand her daughter's anger.' **JENNY**

After much discussion, most people seem to agree that it's time to stop sharenting when your children are about 12 or 13. The pictures can be so embarrassing and they're out there forever. Where do you stand on this issue?

READING

1 **Work in pairs. Look at the photos and the title of the article. What do you think 'sharenting' is?**

2 3.03 **Read and listen to the article to check your ideas.**

3 **Read the article and the comments again. Who said or did these things? Write the name.**

1. ______________ had previously discussed the issue of sharenting with her mother.
2. ______________ made the decision to continue sharenting against her daughter's wishes.
3. ______________ said parents should think carefully before they share.
4. ______________ thinks it was OK to share some pictures and not others.
5. ______________ thinks it's OK to sharent when very few people will see the photos.
6. ______________ thinks parents should respect their children's wishes.

4 SPEAKING **Work in pairs and discuss the questions.**

1. Have your parents ever shared a photo of you that you wish they hadn't?
2. What are your opinions on sharenting? Do you think parents should ask for your consent before posting a picture on Instagram or on other social media?

SPEAKING

5 **Read each sentence and choose a number from 1–5 (1 = I strongly agree, 5 = I strongly disagree.)**

1. Teenagers should always be supported by their parents. 1 2 3 4 5
2. Parents are not the most important people in teenagers' lives. 1 2 3 4 5
3. Parents should give teenagers freedom of choice in everything. 1 2 3 4 5
4. Teenagers should spend as much time as possible with parents/family. 1 2 3 4 5

6 **Discuss your answers in groups. Which question(s) do almost all of you agree on? And which one(s) do almost all of you disagree on? Why?**

GRAMMAR
so and *such* (review)

7 Write the correct words to complete the sentences. Check in the article on page 34, then complete the rule with *so* and *such*.

1 I was ______________ embarrassed.
2 It was ______________ a bad picture.

> **RULE:** We use *so* and *such* to emphasise.
> [3] ________________________ (*a*/*an*) + (adjective) + noun
> [4] ________________________ + adjective
> We often follow *so* and *such* with a *that* clause to talk about consequences.
> *It was such a difficult question that I didn't know what to say.*
> *It was so hot that I couldn't sunbathe.*

8 Complete the sentences with *so* or *such* and your own ideas.

0 It was ___*such*___ a hot day that *we stopped working and went to the beach*.
1 The homework was ______________ difficult that …
2 He's ______________ a good friend that …
3 The train was ______________ late that …
4 It was ______________ an exciting book that …

→ workbook page 28

do and *did* for emphasis

9 Complete the sentences from the article on page 34 with the missing word, then read the rule.

1 I ______________ understand her daughter's anger.
2 She ______________ ask her mother if the content could be taken down, but her mother refused.

> **RULE:** We can use the auxiliaries *do*, *does*, *did* to add emphasis to what we want to say, often when we're contradicting someone.
> **A:** *You didn't like the film, did you?*
> **B:** *I did like it!*
> **A:** *She doesn't want to go to the party.*
> **B:** *She does want to go – she's just shy.*

> **Look**
> ***too* and *not enough***
> To say something is more than we need, we use *too*, and to say that it's less, we use *not enough*.
> *too* + adjective
> *too* + *many* + countable noun
> *too* + *much* + uncountable noun
> *not* + *adjective* + enough

10 Complete the second sentence so it has a similar meaning to the first, using the word given and *so*/*such*, *did* for emphasis or *too*/*not enough*. Write between two and five words.

1 There were too many people at the meeting. Some people had to stand.
There ________________________ at the meeting, so some people had to stand. (chairs)
2 He spends too much money.
He ________________________ money. (save)
3 This book isn't interesting enough. I'm not going to finish it.
This book is ________________________ finish. (boring)
4 You're wrong. I thought the book was really, really good.
I ________________________ the book. (like)

→ workbook page 29

> **PRONUNCIATION**
> Adding emphasis Go to page 120.

VOCABULARY
Bringing up children

11 Complete the phrases in the text with the words in the list.

bring | childhood | do (x2) | get | grow | soft | strict

The toughest job in the world

Most parents want to [1]________________ *their best* for their children and help them [2]________________ *ahead in life*. They try to [3]________________ their children *up* well and give them a happy [4]________________. But it's not always so easy. Children [5]________________ *up* so fast these days and it can be difficult to get it right all the time. Of course, parents know the importance of school and they want their children to [6]________________ *well*, but what happens when the child doesn't want to try? If they are too [7]________________, their children might rebel. If they are too [8]________________, then the children might only do the things they want to do. It's a difficult balancing act and, of course, parents get it wrong sometimes. After all, they're only human.

12 Match phrases 1–8 from Exercise 11 with their meanings.

a ☐ make advances in life
b ☐ raise
c ☐ get older
d ☐ be a success
e ☐ to describe a parent who has very few (or no) rules
f ☐ be as good as you can
g ☐ to describe a parent who has lots of rules
h ☐ the time of being a child

→ workbook page 30

Literature

1 Look at the poster and then read the introduction to the extract. Who do you think the people on the poster are?

2 🔊 3.06 Read and listen to the extract. What two choices does Marcus have?

About a Boy by Nick Hornby

Marcus is a schoolboy who lives with his mum, who is depressed. Marcus has a hard time at school – he gets bullied quite a lot, especially because of the clothes his mum makes him wear. Recently, Marcus has started to become friends with Will, a rich, lazy man who buys him new trainers. Here, Marcus and his mum are going home after visiting Will at his flat.

'You're not going round there again,' she said on the way home.

Marcus knew she'd say it, and he also knew that he'd take no notice, but he argued anyway.

'Why not?'

'If you've got anything to say, you say it to me. If you want new clothes, I'll get them.'

'But you don't know what I need.'

'So tell me.'

'I don't know what I need. Only Will knows what I need.'

'Don't be ridiculous.'

'It's true. He knows what things kids wear.'

'Kids wear what they put on in the mornings.'

'You know what I mean.'

'You mean that he thinks he's trendy, and that [...] he knows which trainers are fashionable, even though he doesn't know the first thing about anything else.'

That was exactly what he meant. That was what Will was good at, and Marcus thought he was lucky to have found him.

'We don't need that kind of person. We're doing all right our way.'

Marcus looked out of the bus window and thought about whether this was true, and decided it wasn't, that neither of them were doing all right, whichever way you looked at it.

'If you are having trouble, it's nothing to do with what shoes you wear, I can tell you that for nothing.'

'No, I know, but –'

'Marcus, trust me, OK? I've been your mother for twelve years. I haven't made too bad a job of it. I do think about it. I know what I'm doing.'

Marcus had never thought of his mother in that way before, as someone who knew what she was doing. He had never thought that she didn't have a clue either; it was just that what she did with him (for him? to him?) didn't appear to be anything like that. He had always looked on being a mother as straightforward, something like, say, driving: most people could do it, and you could mess it up by doing something really obvious, by driving your car into a bus, or not telling your kid to say please and thank you and sorry (there were loads of kids at school, he reckoned, kids who stole and swore too much and bullied other kids, whose mums and dads had a lot to answer for). If you looked at it that way, there wasn't an awful lot to think about. But his mum seemed to be saying that there was more to it than that. She was telling him she had a plan.

If she had a plan, then he had a choice. He could trust her, believe her when she said she knew what she was doing [...] Or he could decide that, actually, she was off her head [...] Either way it was scary. He didn't want to put up with things as they were, but the other choice meant he'd have to be his own mother, and how could you be your own mother when you were only twelve? He could tell himself to say please and thank you and sorry, that was easy, but he didn't know where to start with the rest of it. He didn't even know what the rest of it was. He hadn't even known until today that there was a rest of it.

3 Read the extract again. Mark the sentences T (true) or F (false). Then correct the false sentences.

1 Will buys Marcus a new jacket. ☐
2 Marcus's mum is very fashion-conscious. ☐
3 Marcus doesn't agree that he and his mum are doing OK. ☐
4 His mother doesn't think she's a good mother. ☐
5 The other kids at school never did anything wrong. ☐
6 Marcus didn't think he was capable of being his own mother. ☐

4 VOCABULARY **Match the highlighted words in the extract with the definitions.**

1 up-to-date with modern fashion
2 do it in a really bad way
3 had no idea
4 no matter how
5 thought
6 silly, stupid
7 crazy
8 simple, not complicated

5 SPEAKING **Work in pairs and discuss the questions.**

1 What do you learn about Marcus in the passage? What is he like?
2 What are your mum and dad good at? Think of the positive things about them.

FUNCTIONS
Emphasising

6 **Add *so, such, do* or *did* to the sentences to make them more emphatic. Make any other necessary changes.**

1 He's a good father.
2 She gets on well with children.
3 She's patient.
4 My dad tried his best.
5 My parents made some mistakes.
6 She's soft on her children.

7 SPEAKING **Work in pairs. Who might be talking to whom in each of the sentences in Exercise 6? What was said before?**

Parents can be really embarrassing sometimes!

Our parents have always been a shoulder to cry on, but now we've reached an age where we want to be more independent. At this stage in our lives, we find some of their actions embarrassing and they find some of our reactions upsetting.

First, let's look at what embarrasses us. Top of my list is dressing differently, which applies to my mum. In fact, my friends think she's cool, but I just wish she would dress like the other mothers. Second on my list is being affectionate in public. My dad is guilty of this. He called out: 'I love you' from the car as he dropped me at the school gate, and all my friends heard him. It was so uncool.

Now, let's look at it from our parents' point of view. Firstly, they have lost an adoring child, who once thought of them as heroes. Secondly, they've spent many years looking after you and now you're rejecting their support. They find this difficult.

To conclude, I think parents should understand that teenagers want to be more independent, and teenagers should understand that parents can feel rejected and that this can be hurtful.

8 WRITING **Choose a sentence from Exercise 6 and develop it into a six-line dialogue. The sentence you choose could appear at the beginning, middle or end.**

9 SPEAKING **Think about someone you know who is really good with children or teenagers. Then talk to your partner about your person. Give examples and use emphasis when you can.**

WRITING
An essay

1 INPUT **Read the essay and find two embarrassing things parents sometimes do and two ways in which having a teenager can be hard for parents.**

____

____

____

____

2 **In pairs, think of more embarrassing things your parents or other people's parents do. Write a list.**

3 ANALYSE **Find these phrases in the essay and match them with their meanings.**

1 a shoulder to cry on
2 guilty of
3 feel rejected
4 being affectionate
5 in public

a has done something wrong/bad
b in front of other people
c showing your love
d feel sad and pushed away
e someone who listens to you and is sympathetic

4 **List some of the ways the author introduces a point.**

First, Top of my list, ____________,
____________, ____________,
____________, ____________,

5 PLAN **You're going to write your own essay about the same topic. Make notes for each of the four paragraphs:**

- a short introduction
- two or three things from your point of view as a teenager
- two or three things from your parents' point of view
- a conclusion, giving your final opinion.

6 PRODUCE **Write your essay: Parents can be really embarrassing sometimes! Use your notes from Exercise 5 (about 200 words).**

4 THE ART OF THINKING

OBJECTIVES

FUNCTIONS: expressing frustration

GRAMMAR: *be/get used to (doing)* vs. *used to (do)*; adverbs and adverbial phrases

VOCABULARY: personality adjectives; common adverbial phrases

Get THINKING

Watch the video and think: are you a creative thinker?

A

B

C

READING

1 **Look at the paintings in photos A and B. Make a list of as many differences between them as you can think of. Then compare with a partner.**

2 SPEAKING **Work in pairs or small groups. Discuss how what you can see in photo C might be connected to the differences between the paintings A and B.**

3 **Read the text quickly and check your ideas from Exercise 2.**

4 **Read the text again. Six phrases have been removed. Choose from A–G the phrase which fits each gap (1–6). There is one extra phrase.**

A without using more colours than they actually needed
B and stop it from drying out
C transforming various aspects of life forever
D when you go from Room 41 to Room 42
E and so painters mostly worked indoors, in studios
F to stop the rest from drying out
G meaning the range of colours available to artists increased dramatically

5 4.01 **Read and listen to the article again. Mark the statements T (true) or F (false). Then correct the false statements.**

1 The National Gallery does not have modern paintings. ☐
2 John Goffe Rand was quite a good painter. ☐
3 Things like animal bladders did not last very long as containers. ☐
4 Most artists were accustomed to the problems with oil paint. ☐
5 Rand used tin for the tubes because it was cheap. ☐
6 Artists using the tubes still had to worry about the paint inside them. ☐
7 Rand's tubes were an important factor in the appearance of impressionism. ☐
8 Rand became rich and famous through his inventions. ☐

6 SPEAKING **Work in pairs and do the following.**

1 On a scale of **1–5**, agree on how impressive you think John Goffe Rand's invention was (**1** = not impressive at all, **5** = brilliant!). Say why your group has given this score.
2 The last sentences says that the tube 'went on to be used in many other ways.' List all of the other ways you can think of.

A big change for artists

The National Gallery in Trafalgar Square in London has a collection of paintings that stretches from hundreds of years ago right up to the present day. You can plan a walk that goes chronologically through the centuries – 16th, 17th, 18th century and so on. As you go through the first rooms, you get used to seeing paintings in dark, heavy colours of brown and black, deep reds and blues, with subjects that are indoors, or else in huge landscapes that were created by imaginative painters. But something happens [1]____________________ in the middle of the 19th century. Suddenly, after about 1845, you start to see paintings with dazzling, bright colours and with vivid outdoor settings. How can this remarkable change be explained?

The answer is twofold. First of all, after the Industrial Revolution, artificial pigments had now begun to be used in paint, [2]____________________. The second reason was the work of a man almost no one has heard of: John Goffe Rand.

Rand was an American, born in 1801 in New Hampshire, but he moved to London when he got married. He was a practical but also a creative man: an inventor and an enthusiastic, competent painter. Like all other painters at the time, he worked mainly with oil paints. The problem with oil paint was how to store it [3]____________________. Painters used to keep the paint in animal bladders, which they could pierce to get the paint out, but these were fragile and short-lived containers. It was almost impossible to move the paint from one place to another or to store it for a long time, [4]____________________. Most artists were used to dealing with this situation, but Rand thought he could do something to improve it.

And so in 1841 he invented … the metal tube. Taking very thin layers of tin (a metal which would not react with the oil paint) he made small tubes into which the paint could be poured. The tube could then be squeezed gently to get out as much paint as the artist needed, and closed again [5]____________________. And they were small and light, so they could be taken wherever the painter wanted. These tubes changed everything for artists. Suddenly, they could go out into wide open spaces, fields, gardens and streets, taking their paint with them and painting what they saw, not worrying about the paint itself.

The art movement known as 'impressionism' partly owes its existence to Rand and his tube. One of the greatest impressionist painters, Renoir, told his son: "… without colours in tubes, there would have been no Cézanne, no Monet, no Sisley or Pissarro, nothing of what people were to call impressionism."

John Rand patented his invention, but never became especially wealthy because of it, even though the tube that he invented went on to be used in many other ways, [6]____________________.

Train to THINK

Lateral thinking

'Lateral thinking' means solving problems by thinking in a creative way. It means not following the obvious line of thinking. Here is an example.

A man is driving down a city street at 25 miles per hour. The speed limit is 30 miles per hour. He passes three cars that are travelling at 20 miles per hour. A police officer stops him and gives him a £100 fine. Why?

If we think too much about the speed, we may not get the answer. What does the situation NOT tell us? It doesn't tell us, for example, what time of day it is – so a possible reason for the £100 fine is that it is night time and the man is driving with no lights on his car. Or another possible reason for the fine is that the street is one-way, and the man is driving the wrong way.

7 SPEAKING **Here are more situations. Work in pairs and discuss possible answers.**

1. A father and son are in a bad car crash. They are both taken to hospital. The son is taken into the operating theatre. The doctor there looks at the boy and says: 'That's my son!' How is this possible?
2. A woman is lying awake in bed. She dials a number on the phone, says nothing, puts the phone down and then goes to sleep. Why?
3. A man lives on the 12th floor of a building. Every morning, he takes the lift down to the entrance and leaves the building. In the evening, he gets into the lift and, if there is someone else in the lift, he goes directly to the 12th floor. If the lift is empty, he goes to the 10th floor and walks up two flights of stairs to his apartment. Why?

GRAMMAR

Grammar video ▶10

be / get used to (doing) vs. *used to* (do)

1 Complete these sentences from the article on page 39 with the words from the list. Then complete the rule by choosing the correct options.

dealing | keep | seeing

1 You get used to _______________ paintings in dark, heavy colours.
2 Painters used to _______________ the paint in animal bladders.
3 Most artists were used to _______________ with this situation.

RULE: We use:
[4]*used to do / be used to doing* to talk about situations that were true in the past but are not true now.
[5]*used to do / be used to doing* to talk about something that is familiar.
[6]*be used to doing / get used to doing* to talk about the process of something becoming familiar.

2 Choose the correct words.

1 In the past, people used to *make / making* roads from earth.
2 The roads were bumpy, but people got used to *travel / travelling* on them.
3 Before cars, people used to *travel / travelling* in horse-drawn carriages.
4 The streets in cities used to *be / being* very dirty and smelly.
5 Many people are used to *see / seeing* roads being repaired.
6 Soon we'll get used to *not have / not having* holes in our roads.

3 Complete with the correct form of *be* or *get*.

1 I'm from Sweden, so I _________ used to cold weather.
2 Did it take you long to _________ used to the food here?
3 I lived in the UK for years, but I never _________ used to driving on the left.
4 I think I'll never _________ used to summer in January!
5 _________ you used to life here now?
6 We didn't like the food in Vietnam at first because we _________ used to it.

4 SPEAKING **Work in pairs and think of these things:**

- two things that both you and your partner used to do
- two things you are used to doing
- two things that you have got used to doing this year.

→ workbook page 36

VOCABULARY

Personality adjectives

5 Which adjective from the list is used in the article to describe John Goffe Rand? Which one is used to describe some artists working indoors? What do they mean? What do the other adjectives mean?

arrogant | bad-tempered | bright | cautious
confident | decisive | dull | imaginative
impatient | organised | practical | responsible

6 Read about these people Jane met at her new school. Tick (✓) the people she likes. Cross (✗) the people she doesn't like. Put a question mark (?) where it isn't clear.

0 Rico gets angry all the time and he complains a lot. He's pretty *bad-tempered*. ☒
1 Barbara understands quickly and has lots of good ideas. She's very _______________. ☐
2 Clara doesn't like taking risks. She's a very _______________ person. ☐
3 Dana's great because she makes her mind up really quickly – a really _______________ girl. ☐
4 Derek never has anything interesting to say – he's so _______________! ☐
5 Imogen always has wonderful ideas – she's very _______________. ☐
6 Ian wants everything and he wants it now! He's pretty _______________. ☐
7 Oscar always knows where things are and what he has to do – he's very _______________. ☐
8 Ria is someone you can trust, who makes good decisions – she's _______________. ☐

7 Complete the gaps in the sentences in Exercise 6 with the words from Exercise 5.

→ workbook page 38

SPEAKING

8 Work in pairs. Think of five different people and write sentences to describe them. Don't include an adjective.

Leah is waiting for her friend, who's two minutes late. She calls her to see where she is.

9 Change partners and read your sentences from Exercise 8. Can they guess the adjective you were thinking of?

impatient

10 Ask your partner extra questions about their adjective.

Do you often get impatient in this kind of situation?

LISTENING

11 SPEAKING **Look at the two tasks. Think of ideas for both. Then compare with a partner.**

How imaginative are YOU?

Try these two tasks to see how **imaginative** you are.

1 Look at these CDs. How many different uses can you think of for old CDs? Make a list of at least six things.

2 Look at the picture. How many different things can you see in it?

1

2

12 4.02 **Lewis and Phoebe did the tasks. Listen and do the following:**

1 Note the things they thought of for the CDs.

2 Note the things they saw in the picture.

13 SPEAKING **In groups, compare Lewis and Phoebe's ideas with your own ideas from Exercise 11.**

14 4.02 **Listen again and complete each sentence with no more than three words.**

1 Lewis says that candles these days ______ .

2 Lewis thinks you can throw the CD and ______ to bring it back.

3 Phoebe isn't really sure if she can ______ in the picture.

4 Phoebe says that Lewis shouldn't be ______ on himself.

5 The two of them are happy that there aren't ______ creative thinking.

6 Lewis says that he doesn't want ______ the magazine now.

TH!NK values

Appreciating creative solutions

15 Choose the best way to finish this sentence.

I think the tasks in Exercise 11 tell us that ...

1 it's important to be imaginative.

2 being imaginative is better than being practical.

3 you can be an imaginative person even if you're not good at these tasks.

4 not everybody is as imaginative as everybody else.

5 everybody's imagination is different.

16 Now put these in order of importance for you (1 = most important, 5 = least important).

☐ being practical
☐ being imaginative
☐ knowing a lot of things
☐ being responsible
☐ being organised

17 SPEAKING **Work in pairs. Compare your answers. How similar are your ideas?**

WordWise: Expressions with *good*

18 Look at these sentences from the unit so far. Complete them with phrases from the list.

for good | it's a good thing | it's no good | ~~not very good at~~ | so far, so good

0 I'm *not very good at* them, so I guess I'm not very imaginative.

1 Yes, three. ______ . But I'm not sure I can think of three more.

2 ______ there aren't any tests on creative thinking, isn't it?

3 But ______ , I can't see anything at all.

4 I'm going to stop buying it ______ .

19 Match the phrases in Exercise 18 with these meanings.

a for ever ☐

b there are no positive results ☐

c I'm / We're / You're lucky that ... ☐

d We have started but not finished, but everything has been OK until now. ☐

e have no talent for ☐

→ workbook page 38

READING

1 **Read the post from Jake on the 'Your answers here' website. What does he want to know?**

I had a problem recently, so I asked a friend to help me. She immediately said, 'Think outside the box.' I've heard that expression so many times, but what does it really mean? And how can you learn to do it? Thanks!

2 SPEAKING **Work in pairs and think of ways to help Jake.**

3 **Read what Soraya replies to Jake. How similar are her ideas to yours?**

4 4.03 **Read and listen to both posts again. Mark the statements T (true) or F (false). Then correct the false statements.**

1. Soraya uses a puzzle to illustrate thinking outside the box. ☐
2. She thinks it isn't very difficult to change how you think. ☐
3. She advises not staying in the same place when you want to think creatively. ☐
4. She thinks you should list ideas but throw out the ones that aren't so good. ☐
5. She says that Jake should write and sell articles. ☐
6. She believes that doing a lot of different kinds of thinking makes us better thinkers. ☐
7. She thinks that it can be useful to talk to older people. ☐
8. She thinks children often know the right answer. ☐

5 SPEAKING **Work in pairs and discuss the questions.**

1. Do you think Soraya's answer is helpful? Why (not)?
2. Which of her tips do you like most? Which do you like least?

PRONUNCIATION
Pronouncing words with *gh* Go to page 120.

WRITING
A story

6 **Write a story. The story must start with these words:**

'I had no idea what to do.'

Write 150–200 words.

HOME NEW POSTS ARCHIVES

Hi Jake,

Great question! To understand 'thinking outside the box', we need to start by asking what the 'box' is. We can demonstrate this in an interesting way by looking at the puzzle here.

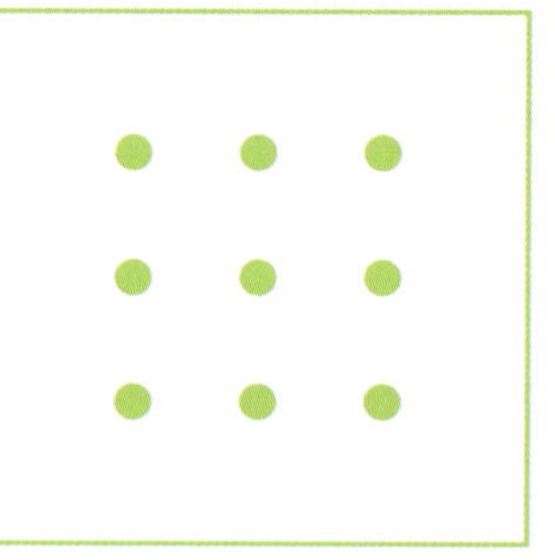

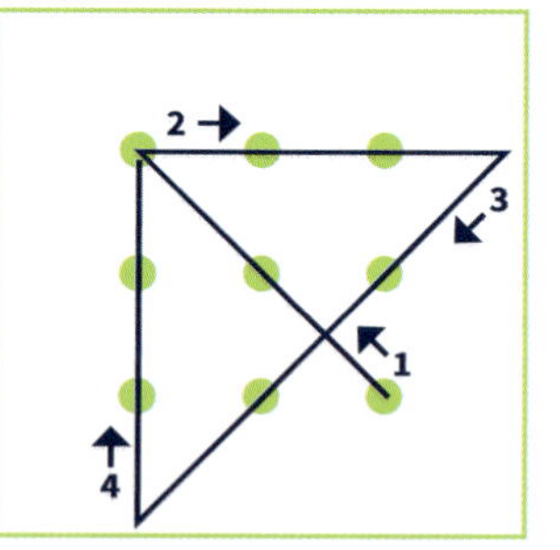

You have to join all nine points, using only four lines and not lifting the pen from the paper. In the answer, the idea of 'outside the box' is illustrated nicely. No one said you have to stay inside the 'box' of the nine points, but if you do, you can't solve the problem. Go 'out of the box' and you can solve it easily.

So, thinking outside the box means moving away from your usual way of thinking. It means thinking creatively, thinking in a different way. Now, what about tips on how to do it?

Changing your way of thinking isn't easy; you have to work hard at it. But it can be done. My first tip is, if you're a bit stuck – get out of your box, physically. Leave the room, go for a walk, take a shower, run – anything that takes you away from that paper or screen in front of you. Steve Jobs did it, so did Tchaikovsky, and most likely many other successful people.

Secondly: try brainstorming, i.e. thinking of as many alternatives as you can without judging or evaluating them. Imagine you want to earn some money – you'll probably think of things you could do like washing cars or working in people's gardens. But sit down and make a list of other things people do that can make money – write articles for online publications, make lemonade and sell it to passers-by, whatever. Open your mind completely, and you could find some great answers.

Thirdly, in order to think creatively, you need to do a lot of, well … thinking! Play word games, do puzzles like Sudoku, anagrams, crosswords, whatever you prefer. Like a muscle, the more you use it, the stronger your brain becomes. You can also give yourself challenges like thinking of different uses for household objects (books, old shoes, plates you don't want any more): it trains you to look at things from a different angle. So, make sure you train your brain!

Last but not least – talk to a lot of people, including kids. Older people have experience that could help you think of something you would never think of. Kids can think outside the box because they're too young to know what the box is. Have fun!

GRAMMAR
Adverbs and adverbial phrases

7 **For each sentence, put a letter in the box to say if the underlined adverb is an adverb of time (T), manner (M), place (P) or certainty (C).**

0 Open your mind completely. [M]
1 I read about it recently. [ ]
2 This is definitely the best album they've ever made. [ ]
3 He'll probably win the prize. [ ]
4 You can buy most of the things you need locally. [ ]
5 You are capable of thinking creatively. [ ]
6 We got home at nine o'clock. [ ]
7 This is possibly the best work I've ever done. [ ]
8 You can choose the best ideas later. [ ]
9 I applied for the course, and, surprisingly, they accepted me! [ ]

8 **Look back at the posts on page 42. What verbs do these words qualify?**

1 immediately
2 easily
3 creatively
4 hard
5 completely

9 **Sometimes we use adverbial phrases instead of an adverb. Add the words below to lists A and B. Then choose the correct words to complete the rule.**

enthusiasm | fear | friendly | interesting | strange | surprise

A	B
in an enjoyable way	with / without difficulty
in a horrible way	with / without excitement
in a different way	with / without interest
in a [1] _______ way	with / without [4] _______
in an [2] _______ way	with / without [5] _______
in a [3] _______ way	with / without [6] _______

RULE: We often form adverbial phrases with:
- *in a/an* + [7] *noun / adjective* + *way*
- *with/without* + [8] *noun / adjective*

10 **Complete the sentences. Use phrases from Exercise 9. Sometimes more than one answer is possible.**

1 I really like music, so I went to the concert with …
2 The first time I met her, she looked at me in …
3 The run was easy – I finished it without …
4 Some of the people at the party were dressed in …
5 It was a great documentary and I watched it with …
6 I don't really like sport, so I went to the match without …

→ workbook page 37

VOCABULARY
Common adverbial phrases

11 **Use the words from the list to complete the definitions.**

by accident | in a hurry | in a panic | in a row | in private | in public | ~~in secret~~ | on purpose

If you do something …
0 without other people knowing, you do it *in secret* .
1 that other people can hear or see, you do it _______ .
2 that other people can't hear or see, you do it _______ .
3 that you intended to do, you do it _______ .
4 that you didn't want to do, you do it _______ .
5 feeling stressed and without thinking properly, you do it _______ .
6 quickly, you do it _______ .
7 three times without a break, you do it three times _______ .

12 **Choose the correct words.**

1 The two of us went into a room, alone, so that we could talk *in a hurry / in private*.
2 He broke my phone and I'm really angry. I'm sure he did it *on purpose / in a panic*.
3 You shouldn't have behaved that way *in public / in private*. Everyone was staring.
4 I woke up late four days *in a row / in secret*!
5 I was very late, so I had to leave the house *on purpose / in a hurry*.
6 He was *in secret / in a panic* because he couldn't find his mobile phone.
7 I'm so sorry that I lost your papers – I left them on the bus *on purpose / by accident*.
8 She did it late at night *in secret / in a panic*. No one knew anything.

13 SPEAKING **Work in pairs and discuss the questions.**

1 When were you last in a hurry?
2 What can you do five times in a row?
3 Give an example of something you did on purpose and wish you hadn't.
4 Give an example of something you got right by accident.
5 When was the last time you were in a panic?

→ workbook page 38

DEVELOPING SPEAKING

1 4.06 **Look at the photo. How do you think Paulo is feeling? Read and listen to check.**

Paulo: This is terrible. The teacher told us she wants us to write something creative! 'A poem about the natural world.' How am I going to do that? And she wants it by Tuesday! No chance!

Sarah: Calm down, Paulo! All you need is one idea.

Paulo: That's just it – I don't have any ideas. Not one! I'm hopeless at this kind of thing. I could sit and think for days, but it's pointless. I'll never come up with anything.

Alex: Oh, give it a rest Paulo! You're always putting yourself down. 'I can't do this, I'm no good at that!' It's really boring!

Sarah: Hang on, Alex. That's a bit out of order. We're supposed to be helping him, not making him feel worse. It would be nice if you could be a bit more supportive!

Paulo: No, he's right. I *am* being boring. And bad-tempered, too.

Sarah: Whatever. Let's think. You've got to write a poem about … what was it again?

Paulo: 'The natural world'. But listen, guys, it's my problem, not yours. You don't have to help me.

Sarah: But we want to! Well, I want to, at least. Look, I always think it's useful to try to think outside the box.

Alex: Oh, Sarah! 'Think outside the box?' That's such a cliché.

Paulo: No, she might be right. I mean, perhaps … instead of writing a poem *about* nature, I could write something from nature's point of view.

Sarah: Like, a poem written by the ocean, about having plastic bags floating around inside it.

Alex: Oh, no! You can't be serious, Sarah!

Paulo: It's a good idea! I'll call it: 'I am the ocean'.

Alex: Good luck Paulo – you're going to need it!

2 4.06 **Read and listen to the dialogue again and answer the questions.**

1 What does Paulo have to do?
2 Why does Alex get irritated by Paulo?
3 Why does Alex get irritated by Sarah?
4 What is the idea Sarah gives Paulo?

3 SPEAKING **Work in pairs. Say how you felt about each person in the conversation.**

Phrases for fluency

4 Find the underlined expressions in the dialogue and use them to complete the conversations.

1 Sorry, I've forgotten. What's your name ______________________ ?

2 A Let's go for a run.
B A run? You ______________________ ! It's really cold out there!

3 A Come on, we're late!
B ______________________ , we're not late at all, we've got another fifteen minutes.

4 A That shirt doesn't suit you.
B Oh, ______________________ , Boris. I'm tired of you criticising me all the time. You're really ______________________ , you know?

5 A Let's watch a film on TV – if there's anything good.
B ______________________ . The films on TV are terrible!

5 SPEAKING **Work in groups of three. You are Paulo, Sarah and Alex. Paulo has written his poem and the teacher has graded it. Sarah and Alex talk to him to find out more.**

FUNCTIONS
Expressing frustration

KEY LANGUAGE

I can't (do that).
I'm hopeless (at …)
This is hopeless!
No chance.
I give up.
I'll never (come up with anything).
(It's) pointless.

6 Read the conversation again. Which phrases from the Key Language box does Paulo not say? What do all the phrases have in common?

7 WRITING **Think of a frustrating situation you have been in. Write three things you might have thought using the phrases in Exercise 6. Compare your notes with a partner.**

I'll never finish this.

LIFE COMPETENCIES

Sometimes people need our understanding and support, even if what they see as a problem is not something we ourselves think is serious or important.

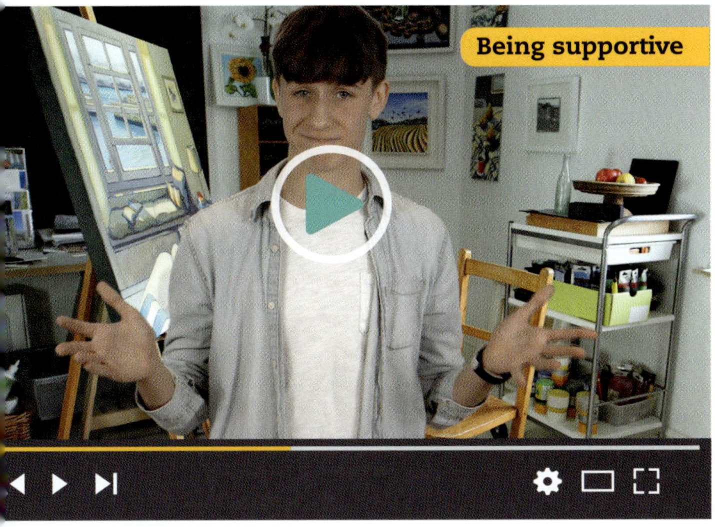

1 ▶ 11 **Watch the vlog. Answer the questions.**

1 What is Will's problem?
2 What is his solution?

2 ▶ 11 **Watch the vlog again. Work in pairs and think of two other ways Will could show Max some support.**

3 **Read these situations. For each situation, choose the best response.**

1 A friend of yours has reached the final of a local table-tennis tournament. Unfortunately, she broke her bat and she is really worried about using a borrowed one.
   A Don't worry – you've done well to reach the final, so it doesn't matter if you lose.
   B You're such a good player – I'm sure you'll do well with any bat.
   C Why is the bat such a big deal? Aren't they all basically the same?

2 You invite a friend to join you and other friends to go out. Your friend says, 'Sorry, I can't. I've got so much homework to do. I need to finish it tonight.'
   A You've got another two days. Come out with us!
   B OK, but why don't you come with us and relax? And I can help you tomorrow.
   C You take schoolwork too seriously. You've got to have fun sometimes.

3 It's your friend's mum's birthday soon. He wants to get her something nice, but he hasn't got much money. You know he bought a new tablet recently.
   A I can lend you some money, but perhaps you should think more carefully about how you spend your money.
   B Well, it's your own fault. You shouldn't have bought that tablet.
   C Just buy something with what you've got. Your mum won't be expecting anything fancy.

4 SPEAKING **Work in pairs or small groups. A friend says these things. Think of something supportive to say in reply.**

'I'm feeling awful. I promised my grandma I'd go for a walk with her, but now I've got to stay at home and help my brother with something. I'll have to phone Grandma and tell her I can't come. I hate doing this!'

'My sister's being a real pain. She argues with me all the time and says things she knows I don't like. She laughs at everything I do, too. But my parents think she's so sweet!'

Me and my world

5 **Think of a time when someone said something very supportive to you and make notes.**

- What was the problem?
- Who was the person? What did they say?
- Why did you think it was supportive?

6 SPEAKING **Work in pairs and tell your partner your ideas from Exercise 5.**

TIPS FOR BEING SUPPORTIVE

- When you are listening to other people's problems, try not to judge them or the problem.
- You don't have to solve the problem – just try to say something that shows you understand.
- Try to put yourself in the other person's position. What would you like to hear?

B2 First for Schools

LISTENING

Part 1: Multiple choice

→ workbook page 79

1 4.07 **You will hear people talking in eight different situations. For questions 1–8, choose the best answer (A, B or C).**

1 You hear two people talking at a theatre.
Why has the man never been to the theatre before?
A It's too expensive.
B He hated plays at school.
C He prefers films.

2 You hear a voicemail message.
What is the reason Julia called?
A to invite Sally to her party
B to ask Sally about a party in Germany
C to say that Ralf needs Sally's phone number

3 You hear two people talking about a restaurant.
What problem does the woman mention?
A the quality of the food
B the slow waiters
C the high prices

4 You hear an actor talking about his latest film.
Why was he pleased to be given this role?
A His part is different from what he's done recently.
B He had forgotten what it was like to be in a film.
C People will know that he's good at playing bad guys.

5 You hear a woman talking on the radio.
What kind of broadcast is it?
A an advertisement for a supermarket
B a shopping programme
C a programme about healthy eating

6 You hear part of a radio phone-in.
What is the man complaining about?
A his neighbours
B the roads
C his taxes

7 You hear the manager of a football team after the match.
What is she disappointed about?
A the weather
B the referee
C the score

8 You overhear a man talking about his holiday.
What did he like most about it?
A how quiet the location was
B not receiving phone calls
C being near birds and trees

Part 3: Multiple matching

→ workbook page 35

2 4.08 **You will hear five short extracts in which people are talking about an after-school art club. Choose from the list (A–H) what each speaker likes most about the club. Use the letters only once. There are three extra letters which you do not need to use.**

A Practising different forms of art is enjoyable.
B It's a good opportunity to meet people with the same interest.
C It's a welcome break from academic subjects.
D It provides information about future career possibilities.
E It's interesting to find out about painters from other times.
F The teacher is very inspiring.
G The other students are brilliant artists.
H Discovering a new talent is rewarding.

Speaker 1 ☐
Speaker 2 ☐
Speaker 3 ☐
Speaker 4 ☐
Speaker 5 ☐

TEST YOURSELF UNITS 3 & 4

VOCABULARY

1 Complete the sentences with the words in the list. There are four extra words.

accident | bad-tempered | best | grow | helmets | imaginative
organised | panic | public | row | secret | soft | strict | well

1 My parents were quite ____________________ when I was young. I couldn't do everything I wanted to do.
2 My mother was very ____________________ . The house was always tidy with everything in the right place.
3 She always had our school things ready for us, even our cycling ____________________ .
4 I had five brothers and although we were often very difficult, I don't think she was ever ____________________ .
5 Both my parents did everything they could to help us do ____________________ in life.
6 They kept any arguments for when they were alone. They never argued in ____________________ .
7 My dad invented great games for us. He really was very ____________________ .
8 He was very calm. I never saw him in a ____________________ .
9 Once we helped him prepare a surprise party for my mum. Everything had to be done in____________________ so she wouldn't find out.
10 I think we were lucky to ____________________ up in such a family. /10

GRAMMAR

2 Complete the sentences with the words in the list. There are two extra words.

enthusiasm | few | little | live | living | most | none | surprise

1 Josh doesn't like volleyball much, so he went to the volleyball game without much ____________________ .
2 ____________________ of my friends could come to the party. They were all away on holiday.
3 When I was a child, I used to ____________________ in London.
4 Kyle has seen loads of films, but he's only read a ____________________ books.
5 Penny has never got used to ____________________ away from her family.
6 Samya wanted to spend a ____________________ more time on practising her speech.

3 Find and correct the mistake in each sentence.

1 The test was such difficult that nobody got everything right.
2 Khaled was used to be alone in the old house so he wasn't worried.
3 Sara was much scared to stay there after dark.
4 Manu listened with interesting to the interview with the local politician.
5 There was hardly any of space on the shelf, so I couldn't put the books there.
6 My grandmother always preferred her laptop. She never used to using a tablet. /12

FUNCTIONAL LANGUAGE

4 Choose the correct options.

1 A *I'll never / give up* write a novel.
B Don't be *so / such* pessimistic! I'm sure you can do it.
2 A But you're *so / such* a good writer. Can't you write one for me?
B *No chance / I can't* do that – but I'll help.
3 A Oh, dear! This project is *so / such* difficult.
B What's the problem? You're usually *so / such* an imaginative person.
4 A Oh! I'm *give up / hopeless* at drawing. This dog looks more like a bear!
B Come on! Don't get *so / such* angry! Why don't you find a dog on the internet and copy it? /8

MY SCORE /30

22–30 | 10–21 | 0–9

5 TOO MUCH TECH?

Get THINKING

Watch the video and think:
what type of technology is most important to you?

OBJECTIVES

FUNCTIONS:
advice and obligation

GRAMMAR:
obligation, permission and prohibition (review); necessity: *didn't need to / needn't have*; ability in the past (*could, was / were able to, managed to, succeeded in*)

VOCABULARY:
technology (nouns); technology (verbs)

READING

1 **What types of personal technology can you see in the photos? What other technological items do you use? Make a list.**

2 SPEAKING **Work in pairs and choose three items from your lists. Think of some advantages and disadvantages each of the items may have.**

3 5.01 **Read and listen to the article. Discuss the questions.**

1 Which of the statistics do you find most interesting? Why?
2 Which piece of advice do you find most useful? Why?

4 **Read the article again. Match the tips with the titles. There are four extra titles.**

A Be realistic
B Let others know about your plans
C Focus on others
D Don't change your phone for the latest model
E Leave your phone at home
F Get a good night's sleep
G Make a list
H Don't text it – say it instead!
I Start tomorrow
J It's easier with a friend
K One goal at a time

5 SPEAKING **Work in pairs and discuss the questions.**

1 Do you think you use too much technology? Explain your reasons.
2 What other advice would you give to someone who wants to try and use their phone less?

A DIGITAL detox

On average, we look at our phones 200 times a day. That's more than 12 times for every hour we're awake! A quarter of all people spend more time on their phone than they do asleep in bed. Nearly three-quarters of teenagers prefer texting to actually speaking with other people and, presumably, most of those teens also think that having a good wireless router in the house is more important than having a fridge. On average, a teenager will send 3,400 messages from their bed each month!

These are just a few of the frightening statistics that show how addicted we have become to technology. And the effects of this are just as scary. Research has shown that our intensive phone usage means we are finding it harder to get a good night's sleep. Our addiction to social media means we are becoming more self-absorbed and screens are making our children less caring people, as they are less likely to think about the impact of what they might post on social media. Clearly, we must do something about this. But what?

More and more experts are recommending a digital detox – an amount of time every day when we don't allow ourselves to look at our phones and other screens. Most people would probably agree this is a good idea, but putting it into practice is not that easy. That's why we've come up with a seven-step plan to help you put away your phone and get back to the business of living your life.

1 ____________________

Write down all the things that you like doing but never find the time to do. By cutting down your online activity you will start to free up some time to do these things.

2 ____________________

Don't expect to be able to just put down your phone and never touch it again. Instead give yourself a time limit of how long you can use it each day. Even better, say exactly when you will allow yourself to use it and stick to that plan.

3 ____________________

Decide on one change you want to make. Always leave your charger at home, so that you have to use your phone less to save the battery, and work towards achieving this. When you're comfortable with that change, move onto another.

4 ____________________

When you're with others, you should always give them your attention. If you keep looking at your phone, then you are not. This is a sign that it's time to start putting your phone away.

5 ____________________

Find someone to start your detox with. That way, you can offer each other support and help each other through those difficult times. And if you need help, try and talk to them face to face rather than via text or video calls.

6 ____________________

It's simple. If you haven't got your phone with you, then you can't use it. Don't be scared – you'll soon find lots of other things to do. You may even start to notice things you never noticed before.

7 ____________________

Tell friends and family members what you're doing. Let them know you won't always be answering their messages the minute you get them. Who knows – they might even be tempted to join you.

Train to THINK

The PMI strategy

A good brainstorming strategy you can use when making decisions is the PMI strategy. On a piece of paper, draw three columns and head them 'plus', 'minus' and 'interesting'. Write down the positive consequences (plus) and negative consequences (minus) of taking the decision, and also what would be 'interesting' about carrying it out.

6 **Look at the example below. Can you think of any more ideas for each column?**

Phones should be banned from schools		
plus	minus	interesting
Students would focus more on their lessons.	*Students wouldn't be able to communicate with parents if they needed to.*	*How would this change teachers' lives?*

7 SPEAKING **Work in groups and choose one of these situations. Use the PMI strategy to come to a decision.**

- Your group has been asked to take part in a reality TV show. It involves living without any technology for a month. You are not sure whether you should take part.
- Your group has been invited to make a recommendation to the public transport service of your town as to whether mobile phones should be forbidden on buses, trains and trams.
- Your group has been asked to make a report on whether mobile phones should only be used by people over 18.

GRAMMAR

Obligation, permission and prohibition (review)

1 **Complete the sentences from the text on page 49. Then complete the rule with *let, must, should, need to* and *not be allowed to*.**

1 Clearly, we ____________________ do something about this.

2 When you're with others, you ____________________ always give them your attention.

> **RULE:** To express obligation or necessity, we can use *have to* or [3]____________________ (as in sentence 1).
>
> - To say something is (or isn't) a good idea, we can use [4]____________________ (as in sentence 2).
> - To express no obligation or necessity, we can use *don't have to* or *don't* [5]____________________.
> - To express permission, we can use [6]____________________ and to say that something is not permitted we use [7]____________________.

Look

- *had better* = something is a good idea and is often used as a warning. The form is always *had better* + the base form of verb, even when talking about the present.
- *be supposed to* = there's an obligation to do something, but in reality, people don't always do it. It is always used in the passive form (like *be allowed to*).

2 **Complete the second sentence so that it has a similar meaning to the first sentence. Use the word in brackets. Use between two and five words including the word given.**

1 Their son can't go out after 8 pm. (allowed)
Their son ____________________ go out after 8 pm.

2 Our teacher expects us to put up our hand if we want to ask a question. (supposed)
We ____________________ put up our hand if we want to ask a question.

3 Their young daughter isn't allowed to watch TV all day. (let)
They ____________________ their young daughter watch TV all day.

4 You should really turn off the TV if you don't want to get a headache. (better)
You ____________________ off the TV if you don't want to get a headache.

→ workbook page 46

FUNCTIONS

Advice and obligation

3 WRITING **Imagine an exchange student is coming to your school for a few weeks. Write down three rules and three pieces of advice to help them.**

You have to arrive at school by 9 am.

4 SPEAKING **Work in pairs and compare your sentences.**

VOCABULARY

Technology (nouns)

5 **Match the words with the photos. Write the numbers in the boxes.**

> 1 adapter | 2 'at' symbol | 3 charger | 4 headset
> 5 plug | 6 power lead | 7 protective case
> 8 USB port | 9 webcam | 10 wireless router

A

B

C

D

E

F

G

H

I

J

6 **Complete the sentences using the words from Exercise 5.**

1 There's something wrong with that email address. There's no ____________________ in it.

2 I forgot to bring a UK ____________________, so I couldn't plug in my laptop.

3 I left the ____________________ for my phone at home and I'm almost out of battery. Can I borrow yours?

4 You can't get a wi-fi signal? Have you checked if the ____________________ is switched on?

5 My laptop's only got one ____________________, so I can't plug in my mouse and my phone at the same time.

6 I couldn't use my laptop. I left the ____________________ at home and it was out of battery.

7 I'm going to plug in my ____________________. I don't want everyone to hear what you're saying.

8 It's the wrong ____________________. You need an adaptor.

→ workbook page 48

LISTENING

7 Look at the photo. What do you think this invention does?

8 5.02 **Listen to the podcast to check your ideas.**

9 5.02 **Listen again and complete the sentences.**

1 Sian says that Aaron has a really bad ______________ .

2 Dominic Wilcox was ______________ from *The Wizard of Oz*.

3 The GPS system is in ______________ .

4 The left shoe shows you ______________ .

5 The right shoe shows you ______________ .

6 The shoes communicate with each other ______________ .

GRAMMAR

Grammar video ▶13

Necessity: *didn't need to / needn't have*

10 Look at the examples from the listening and answer the questions. Then complete the rule with *didn't need to do* or *needn't have*.

I needn't have downloaded that GPS app for my phone.

They're so simple to use that I didn't need to read the manual.

1 Did Aaron download a GPS app for his phone?

2 Did Sian read the manual?

RULE: When we use [3] ______________ , it means that someone did something but in fact it wasn't necessary.
When we use [4] ______________ , it often means that someone didn't do something because it wasn't necessary.

11 Choose the correct sentence (A or B) to follow sentences 1–6. You must use all of the sentences.

1 Dad cooked a big meal for us, but we'd already eaten.

2 Dad came and ate with us at the restaurant.

A He needn't have cooked.

B He didn't need to cook.

3 I spent ages doing my homework last night and now Mr Peters isn't here to take it in.

4 Mr Peters told us we had a choice about whether to do the homework or not.

A I didn't need to do it.

B I needn't have done it.

5 She took her umbrella, but it was a really sunny day.

6 The forecast said that it was going to be a lovely sunny day. So she left her umbrella at home.

A She didn't need to take it.

B She needn't have taken it.

→ workbook page 47

VOCABULARY

Technology (verbs)

12 Rewrite the sentences, replacing the words in *italics* with the correct form of the phrases in the list.

to browse the internet | to plug (a laptop) in
to sync devices | to post an update
to save (a document) | to stream (a video)
to connect to the wi-fi | to upgrade (your system)

1 Jack's *watching* yesterday's match *on the internet without downloading it.*

2 I can't *access the internet without using a cable.* There's no signal here.

3 I'm a bit bored so I'm *looking at various websites on the internet.*

4 I think you should spend some money *on improving* your operating system. It's very old.

5 You should *make sure different devices (laptop, tablet, etc.) contain the same information* so you've always got a backup.

6 The printer's not working. Oh! It's not *connected to the electricity supply.*

7 Mia hasn't *added any new content to her vlog* for a week. I hope she's OK.

8 Sam is always losing files because he often forgets to *store* information *on an electronic device.*

→ workbook page 48

SPEAKING

13 Work in pairs. Discuss the questions.

1 How often do you post updates on social media?

2 Which devices do you sync?

3 What was the last TV programme you streamed?

PRONUNCIATION
The schwa /ə/ sound Go to page 120.

Great success for teenage teachers – when silver surfers get connected

A new documentary called *Silver Surfers* shows the inspiring story of a group of teens helping elderly people to improve the quality of their lives by teaching them how to make use of the internet. The people were aged between 76 and 93.

Rosemary Raynes, the director of the documentary, got the idea for the film while talking to her sisters Poppy and Amy about a project the two of them had started several years before in Kingston, Canada. The two teenagers and a group of friends had a clear goal: they wanted to help elderly people to feel more connected to other people, through the use of the internet.

They started the project after witnessing how the internet had changed their own grandparents' lives. Their grandparents could use the internet at a basic level, but wanted to become more proficient. After the two girls had given them a few basic IT lessons, they were able to use the computer confidently, and became enthusiastic users of Skype, Facebook and email.

The two students were so motivated by that success that they got several of their friends to join them. Together, they started to visit a local home for elderly people. Many of the people there couldn't even switch on a computer without help. But the young people were amazed by how much they had learned after only a few lessons.

It's fascinating to see how the silver surfers featured in the film all had very different interests. Some of them wanted to use Facebook to stay in touch with family members who had emigrated to countries as far away as Australia. Others were keen to get ideas for travelling, learning how to play an instrument or cooking.

The outcomes of the project were amazing: 89-year-old Sheila, together with a friend, managed to create a YouTube cooking tutorial; 93-year-old Marilyn succeeded in making a rap video; Albert, 89, initially wanted to learn how to use the web to find old friends, and in doing so he was struck by how easy it was to reconnect online with people he hadn't seen in decades. He even managed to use his newly acquired skills to reunite with his daughter, who he had lost touch with.

The documentary has been met with great enthusiasm in several countries, and a number of follow-up projects have been launched. They are all aimed at helping elderly people to explore the benefits of technology, have fun and stay in touch with others – thanks to a wonderful initiative by two teenage girls.

READING

1 SPEAKING **Work in pairs. Look at the photo and answer the questions.**
   1 What do you think the relationship between the people is?
   2 What do you think they are doing?

2 **Read the article quickly to check your ideas.**

3 5.05 **Read and listen to the article again. Find examples in the article of how elderly people learned to use technology.**

4 **Read the article again and answer the questions.**
   1 What is *Silver Surfers*?
   2 What does it show?
   3 Who started the project?
   4 What inspired them to start the project?
   5 Who did they get to join them?
   6 Where did they start giving lessons?
   7 What were some of the elderly people's interests?
   8 What were some of their achievements?

5 SPEAKING **Work in pairs and discuss the questions.**
   1 What do you think of the *Silver Surfers* project?
   2 Would you be interested in joining such a project? Why (not)?
   3 Which example of the seniors' achievements do you find most impressive?
   4 Have you ever tried to help someone you know with technology? Did you manage to teach them successfully?

GRAMMAR

Ability in the past: *could, was / were able to, managed to, succeeded in*

6 Read the examples from the article on page 52 and then complete the rule with *managed, succeeded, could,* and *couldn't*.

1 Many of the people there couldn't even switch on a computer without help.
2 After [...] a few basic IT lessons, they were able to use the computer confidently.
3 The outcomes of the project were amazing: 89-year-old Sheila [...] managed to create a YouTube cooking tutorial.
4 93-year-old Marilyn succeeded in making a rap video.

RULE: To talk about ability generally in the past we use [5] ________ */couldn't.*
To talk about ability at specific moments in the past, we use *was/were able to* ([6] ________ *to* + infinitive, or [7] ________ *in* + gerund).
To talk about a lack of ability at specific moments in the past, we use [8] ________ */wasn't (weren't) able to.*

7 Choose the correct answers.

1 Her mobile phone broke a week ago. She ___ to access any social networks since then.
A couldn't
B hasn't been able
C hasn't succeeded

2 He was so moved by the award he received that he ___ continue with his speech.
A wasn't able to B succeeded in C could

3 He played football again for the first time after his injury, but he only ___ play for 20 minutes.
A could
B managed to
C succeeded in

4 She had to ask several people until she finally ___ in finding some help.
A managed B succeeded C could

5 My little brother ___ to walk when he was ten months old.
A could
B was able
C succeeded

6 I tried to climb that mountain once, but I ___ to get to the top because of the bad weather.
A couldn't
B didn't succeed
C didn't manage

8 Complete the text with one word for each gap.

When I was eight, my older brother introduced me to a game on his mobile called Geometry Dash. He was brilliant. He [1] ________ complete all the levels. He let me have a go. It was simple. You had to make a little block jump over things by tapping the screen. At first I was terrible. I [2] ________ even jump over the first obstacle. But I kept trying and after about three hours I [3] ________ to complete the first level. I spent the rest of the day playing it and by the end of it I was [4] ________ to do the first three levels. That night in bed, I [5] ________ sleep because I kept on playing Geometry Dash in my head!

9 WRITING Write a short text about some things you couldn't do when you were younger, but that you can do now.

When I was really little, I couldn't ride a bike, but I was able to do it by the time I was five.

→ workbook page 47

SPEAKING

10 You're going to talk about an elderly person who has qualities that you admire. Make notes on why you admire this person.

11 Which of the qualities you have written down would you like to have in your own life?

12 What could you do to develop those qualities?

13 Discuss your ideas with a partner.

TH!NK

Smart cities

Culture

FOUR OF THE SMARTEST CITIES

1 SPEAKING **Work in pairs and decide which of these things you think will be the most important for cities of the future.**

1 caring for old people
2 transport and road congestion
3 cutting down carbon emissions
4 keeping an eye on its citizens
5 reducing the number of inhabitants

2 5.06 **Read and listen to the article. Which of the issues above does it talk about?**

SINGAPORE – AN EYE ON EVERYTHING

Singapore has plans to become the world's first smart country and it is already a nation of sensors. They are everywhere. One area that is highly controlled by the sensors is transport. They are on all buses, trains and taxis and are used to help make sure the traffic runs smoothly. They can also predict where accidents are likely to happen. But the sensors are also used to monitor other areas of Singaporean life. For example, they can detect if someone is dropping litter or smoking in a public place. And for those who are worried about their privacy, the government has promised to make most of the data it collects open to the public, meaning you will be able to access the footage yourself.

SAN FRANCISCO – KEEPING THE TRAFFIC FLOWING

It's not surprising that the new 'capital' of Silicon Valley is also one of the US's smartest cities and it has implemented a number of impressive technologies to make life easier, such as an app that will guide motorists in the city to the nearest free parking spot. This app can detect how many people are in the car and charge accordingly. The more passengers, the cheaper it is. As a result of the tech boom, San Francisco has also seen a big rise in traffic congestion, as more and more people are coming to the city to work. Smart transportation is now a top priority for city planners as they hope to free up their highways and get their citizens moving around more freely.

BARCELONA – GOING GREEN

Barcelona prides itself on being a hub for environmentally-friendly smart technology. It has sensors to help monitor the levels of air and noise pollution and to turn on and off its street lighting, making sure no energy goes to waste. But where Barcelona is really leading the way is with its green technology and measures for reducing carbon emissions. For example, it has a system which checks the water levels in the ground and predicts future rainfall, which allows it to control the city's water consumption more effectively. It also has a smart waste disposal system. Citizens throw their waste into special bins from which it is sucked into underground storage. Here it is sorted and recycled, and some is burned, producing energy for heating systems.

OSLO – TAKING CARE OF THE ELDERLY

Oslo is another city with big green ambitions and it plans to be 95 percent carbon neutral by 2030. However, it also uses smart technology to help take care of its aging population as efficiently as possible. For example, it has installed sensors in the homes of citizens suffering from Alzheimer's disease. The technology allows carers to check in regularly with their patients to make sure all is well. It also reminds the patients of daily tasks, such as taking their medicine, via spoken messages. Motion sensors can also detect whether the patient has left the oven on or left a front door open and send out a warning alarm if the person is in danger. Such technology means more elderly people can continue living in their own homes for longer.

3 Read the article again and answer the questions.

1 How is the Singapore government going to address privacy concerns?
2 How is Barcelona able to manage its water usage more efficiently?
3 What does San Francisco's parking technology do?
4 How do sensors in the home help people with Alzheimer's in Oslo?

4 VOCABULARY **Match the highlighted words in the article with the definitions.**

1 in the quickest and most organised way possible
2 to put an idea into practice
3 overcrowding
4 a centre for something
5 film taken by a camera
6 instruments used to detect something
7 the amount you use something
8 to check and control

5 SPEAKING **Work in pairs and discuss the questions.**

1 What smart technology does your town or city use? Are these initiatives a good idea? Why / Why not?
2 What other types of smart technology would you like to see used in your town or city? Why?

WRITING
Instructions

1 INPUT **Read the instructions on how to save a Word file. Who do you think it has been written for and why?**

One of the most important things you need to learn to do when using a computer to write documents is to learn how to save a file.

1 If your file is a written document, then you will be using a word-processing program such as Microsoft Word. The first thing you need to do is to create a new file. To do this, open up the program by clicking on the icon.
2 When the program has opened, click on the icon 'file' in the top left-hand corner of the screen and choose 'new' from the drop-down menu. This will create a new document for you.
3 I would recommend saving this document before you have written anything. This means that if your computer shuts down unexpectedly, you won't lose the file. To save the file, click on 'file' again. From the drop-down menu, choose 'save'.
4 A dialogue box or window will open asking you to type in the name of your document. You will also need to choose a location for the file. Select 'desktop' from the list on the left-hand side of the box. This means you will be able to find your file easily when you start your computer.
5 Finally, when you close your document, a dialogue box will appear asking if you want to save any changes. Click 'yes' and this will ensure you never lose any of your work.

2 ANALYSE **Complete the sentences. Then read the instructions again to check.**

1 ______________ your file is a written document, ______________ you will be using a word-processing program.
2 The ______________ you need to do is to create a new file.
3 ______________ this, open up the program.
4 ______________ save the file, click on 'file' again.
5 ______________ you will be able to find your file easily.
6 ______________, when you close your document, a dialogue box will appear.

3 **Use a word or phrase from the list to complete each sentence.**

finally | first thing | if
then | this means | to

1 To take photos, the ______________ you need is a camera.
2 ______________ you're serious about photography, ______________ buy the best camera you can afford.
3 Choose a camera with a high number of pixels – ______________ that you'll have good quality images.
4 ______________ find out which are the best cameras, do research on the internet.
5 ______________, start snapping and have fun!

4 PLAN **In pairs, discuss why the following tips are important when writing instructions.**

- Think carefully about who you are writing for.
- Use clear language that is easy to understand.
- Give the instructions in a logical order.
- Use a friendly, informal style.

5 **Choose one of the computing processes below and make notes for each stage.**

- how to create a folder
- how to change the font
- how to cut and paste
- how to rename a file

6 PRODUCE **Write a text (about 200 words) describing the process you chose in Exercise 5. Remember to do these things.**

- Decide who you are writing these instructions for (a child? a beginner? a fairly experienced user?).
- Give your instructions in a logical order.
- Think about the tips from Exercise 4.

6 BETTER TOGETHER

OBJECTIVES

FUNCTIONS: using intensifying comparatives

GRAMMAR: comparatives; linkers of contrast

VOCABULARY: ways of speaking; friendship idioms

Get THINKING

Watch the video and think: what festivals are celebrated in your town or city?

READING

1 SPEAKING **Work in pairs. Look at the photos. What kind of festival do you think these people are attending? How do they feel?**

dull | enthusiastic | excited
miserable | self-confident | terrified

2 SPEAKING **Choose one of the two people and imagine their thoughts. Make notes. Tell your partner the person's thoughts for your partner to guess who it is.**

3 6.01 **Look at the subject line Amy put on her email. Why do you think Amy chose this subject line? Read and listen to the email to check your ideas.**

4 **Read the email again and answer the questions.**

1 What kind of reading material are you most likely to come across at a Comic Con?
2 How can you tell that someone likes the same show as you?
3 Why should Matteo wear a costume?
4 In what way(s) do people connect with each other?
5 How can you enjoy the Casual Cosplay Showcase more?
6 Why does Matteo have to make a quick decision?

5 SPEAKING **Work in pairs and discuss the questions.**

1 Why do you think wearing a costume gives people self-confidence?
2 Have you ever acted in a play or dressed as a superhero? How did it make you feel?
3 In what situations do you feel most self-confident?

The missing suitcase

ROLE PLAY **Work in groups of four. Students A and C: go to page 127. Students B and D: go to page 128.**

Imagine you are going to Comic Con London with three friends. You travelled to London by train. Your suitcase with your costumes in has been lost. Agree together on what you should do.

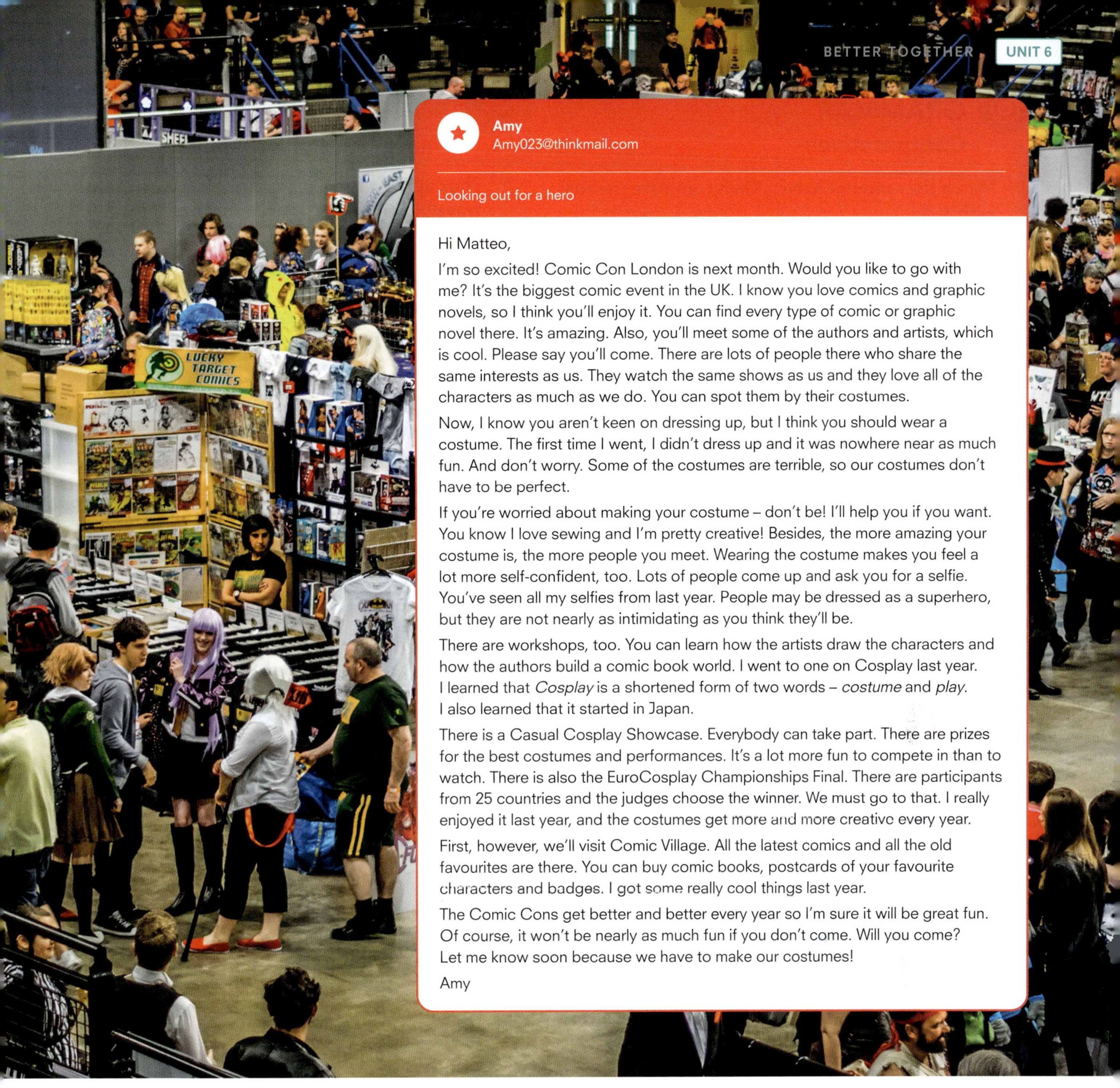

Amy
Amy023@thinkmail.com

Looking out for a hero

Hi Matteo,

I'm so excited! Comic Con London is next month. Would you like to go with me? It's the biggest comic event in the UK. I know you love comics and graphic novels, so I think you'll enjoy it. You can find every type of comic or graphic novel there. It's amazing. Also, you'll meet some of the authors and artists, which is cool. Please say you'll come. There are lots of people there who share the same interests as us. They watch the same shows as us and they love all of the characters as much as we do. You can spot them by their costumes.

Now, I know you aren't keen on dressing up, but I think you should wear a costume. The first time I went, I didn't dress up and it was nowhere near as much fun. And don't worry. Some of the costumes are terrible, so our costumes don't have to be perfect.

If you're worried about making your costume – don't be! I'll help you if you want. You know I love sewing and I'm pretty creative! Besides, the more amazing your costume is, the more people you meet. Wearing the costume makes you feel a lot more self-confident, too. Lots of people come up and ask you for a selfie. You've seen all my selfies from last year. People may be dressed as a superhero, but they are not nearly as intimidating as you think they'll be.

There are workshops, too. You can learn how the artists draw the characters and how the authors build a comic book world. I went to one on Cosplay last year. I learned that *Cosplay* is a shortened form of two words – *costume* and *play*. I also learned that it started in Japan.

There is a Casual Cosplay Showcase. Everybody can take part. There are prizes for the best costumes and performances. It's a lot more fun to compete in than to watch. There is also the EuroCosplay Championships Final. There are participants from 25 countries and the judges choose the winner. We must go to that. I really enjoyed it last year, and the costumes get more and more creative every year.

First, however, we'll visit Comic Village. All the latest comics and all the old favourites are there. You can buy comic books, postcards of your favourite characters and badges. I got some really cool things last year.

The Comic Cons get better and better every year so I'm sure it will be great fun. Of course, it won't be nearly as much fun if you don't come. Will you come? Let me know soon because we have to make our costumes!

Amy

Train to THINK

Exaggeration

When we feel strongly about something, we tend to exaggerate – we call something 'a brilliant idea', 'the best (film) ever', 'an amazing journey', etc. But we often don't mean that literally. As a listener, you need to be aware of exaggeration and understand what the speaker is really saying.

6 Read the example and answer the questions.

Last night's train journey was terrible. It was the worst journey of my life. The train was two hours late and then it stopped for ages in the middle of nowhere. I was so bored I thought I was going to go mad. I hope today's journey won't be as bad.

1 How many exaggerations does the speaker make?
2 What are they?
3 What does he or she really mean in each case?

7 SPEAKING Work in pairs and tell your partner about something really good or really bad that happened to you recently. Use exaggeration.

PRONUNCIATION
Linking words with /dʒ/ and /tʃ/
Go to page 120.

GRAMMAR
Comparatives

1 Match the sentence halves. Then complete the rule with 1–5.

1 The more amazing your costume is, ☐
2 It's a lot more fun to compete in ☐
3 I didn't dress up and it was nowhere near ☐
4 The costumes get more and ☐
5 People are not nearly as ☐

a intimidating as you think they'll be.
b more creative every year.
c the more people you meet.
d than to watch.
e as much fun.

RULE:
A Use *a lot / far / much* + comparative to make a comparative stronger. Sentence [6]__________ .
B Use *just as, not nearly as* and *nowhere near as* + adjective + *as* to intensify a comparison. Sentences [7]__________ and [8]__________ .
C Use comparative *and* comparative + short adjectives e.g. *hotter and hotter* to talk about how something or someone is changing or increasing. Use *more and more* + longer adjectives e.g. *more and more interesting*. Sentence [9]__________ .
D Use *the* + comparative, *the* + comparative with short adjectives or *the more* + adjective, *the more* + adjective + clause with long adjectives to show how two events affect each other. Sentence [10]__________ .

2 Complete the second sentence so that it has a similar meaning to the first. Use the words in brackets. You must use between two and five words, including the word given.

1 Today's test was much easier than yesterday's test. (nowhere)
Today's test was ________________ as yesterday's test.
2 I'm practising the piano a lot and I'm getting much better. (practise)
The more I ________________ I get at playing the piano.
3 I'm sure the price of food is going up each month. (and)
Food is getting ________________ each month.
4 I've been seeing a lot of John recently and I'm beginning not to like him so much. (less)
The more I see John, ________________ I like him.

→ workbook page 54

FUNCTIONS
Using intensifying comparatives

3 Look at what the writer recommends to tourists travelling to the UK. Match the three parts.

1 You should visit Bath.	a *It's easily the best* time to visit.	i And *it's a whole lot* cheaper than the train.
2 You should travel around by bus.	b *It's far and away* the most beautiful city in the UK.	ii And *it's miles less* crowded than London.
3 You should come back in August.	c It's the easiest way to travel *by far*.	iii And *it's even* warmer than it is now.

4 SPEAKING **Make recommendations to visitors to your country, using the sentences in Exercise 3 to help you. Compare your ideas with a partner.**

VOCABULARY
Ways of speaking

5 Which one of these sentences would probably *not* be said about the festival in the email on page 57?

1 'The costumes this year were amazing.'
2 'The first time I went, I didn't make my own costume.'
3 'This man dressed as Iron Man is my friend Jake.'
4 'I think you should enter the Casual Cosplay Showcase.'
5 'The food is terrible.'
6 '*Con* is short for *convention*. It means a large meeting of people for an event.'

6 Match the sentences in Exercise 5 with the speaker's communicative aim.

a to introduce ☐ d to suggest ☐
b to define ☐ e to praise ☐
c to admit ☐ f to criticise ☐

7 Complete the gaps with the suffixes from the list. One word does not have a suffix.

-ion | -ism | -ition | -ssion | -tion

1 to admit — to make an *admission*
2 to introduce — to make an __________
3 to define — to give a __________
4 to suggest — to make a __________
5 to praise — to give __________
6 to criticise — to make a __________

8 Write an example for three of the functions above. Read them to a partner to guess.

You should go and see the new Batman film. It's amazing.

You're making a suggestion.

→ workbook page 56

LISTENING

9 Put the pictures in order to make a story about Carlotta and Lily. Write 1–4 in the boxes.

10 6.04 **Listen to the interview to check your ideas.**

11 6.04 **Listen again and complete the sentences.**

1. In Kindergarten, both Carlotta and Lily wore their hair in ____________________ .
2. If Carlotta was upset, Lily was always a ____________________ to cry on.
3. They were best friends and they did ____________________ together.
4. It was Carlotta's ____________________ that they fell out.
5. Lily was very ____________________ about the fancy-dress competition.
6. Carlotta stole Lily's idea for the ____________________ costume.
7. Lily was the only person who knew that Carlotta couldn't ____________________ .
8. It took quite a long time for Lily to ____________________ Carlotta again.

12 SPEAKING **Work in pairs and answer the questions in pairs.**

1. Do you agree that Lily was right to be angry with Carlotta?
2. Do you understand why Carlotta did what she did?
3. Have you ever had a big fight with a good friend? Are you friends again now?

VOCABULARY
Friendship idioms

13 Match the idioms with the definitions.

1. to look like two peas in a pod ☐
2. to get on like a house on fire ☐
3. to have a shoulder to cry on ☐
4. to bury the hatchet ☐
5. to know someone inside out ☐
6. to be joined at the hip ☐
7. to clear the air ☐
8. to fall out ☐

a to have an argument and not be friends any more
b to do everything together
c to get on with someone really well
d to be so similar that you can't tell one from the other
e to have someone to listen to your problems
f to know somebody very well
g to become friends again after an argument
h to forget the bad feelings between you

14 Complete the story with the correct form of the idioms from Exercise 13.

My identical twin sister, Ana and I [1] ____________________ . People often call me Ana by mistake because we look so similar. As well as looking like each other, we have the same interests, too, and we [2] ____________________ . We spend a lot of time together. We are in the same class at school and we know everything about each other. We [3] ____________________ . When I'm upset, I know I [4] ____________________ . Ana always knows how to cheer me up. We sometimes argue but we have never [5] ____________________ with each other. If we did, I think Ana would be the one to talk things over to [6] ____________________ . She hates arguments and she's always the one to [7] ____________________ and make friends again.
Ana and I do everything together. We are both in the school choir and we both love swimming. My grandma says we're [8] ____________________ .

15 SPEAKING **Work in pairs. Think of some characters in a film or a book who are good friends. Describe their friendship to another pair using the idioms from Exercise 13.**

→ workbook page 56

CoderDojo COOLEST PROJECTS INTERNATIONAL

Every year, kids from all over the world come to the RDS in Dublin to demonstrate the apps, websites, games and hardware projects they have developed in their local Dojo. At the first event in 2012, there were 19 projects and 100 attendees, but in 2018, 10,000 people attended the event, from 114 countries, and 1,000 kids showcased their projects.

Back in 2011, James Whelton, the founder of CoderDojo, set up the first coding club at his school in Cork, in Ireland. He had only just turned 18.

After that, James became well known and was invited to speak at the Dublin Web Summit. He spoke about how he had hacked his iPod Nano to turn it into a watch. James had won the iPod Nano at an awards ceremony, and, bored on the plane on the way home, he had started to play around with it and accidentally hacked it. Then, before he went to bed that night, he wrote about it on his blog. When he woke up, he saw that a quarter of a million people had viewed the blog. After that, all his schoolmates wanted to know how he had done it and asked if he would teach them to code, too. He agreed to set up a coding club at his school and he started to teach basic HTML and CSS to his fellow students. Later that year, he met Bill Liao, an entrepreneur who saw what a great idea this club was. Bill wanted to expand the project to other cities and to other countries, too, and the pair set up CoderDojo.

CoderDojo is run by volunteers and it can be set up anywhere. There is no set curriculum at the clubs. Children from seven to 17 work on what interests them and they learn far more than just coding skills. They also develop problem-solving skills, and learn how to manage a project, work in a team and design something they feel passionate about.

And what's really amazing is that many of the kids' inventions have had a significant social impact. Here are two examples from the event in Dublin:

- The Best International Prize was won by a Romanian team, for their project AZ-Tech Teddy. Their e-health project aims to help prevent childhood obesity. Tech Teddy is a teddy bear for a child to feed and take care of. Children who play with the teddy bear need to track its eating habits carefully. The young coders believe this will teach young children about healthy eating habits.
- Freddie from Wales won the Openet Innovator Prize for his facial recognition door entry system which he designed for elderly people with dementia. 'Safe' people can register their face so that when they come to the door they will be recognised. The system will then tell the homeowner who is at the door and whether to let them in or not.

READING

1 SPEAKING **Work in pairs. Look at the photos and answer the questions.**

1 How do you think the people know each other?
2 Where do you think they are?

2 6.05 **Read and listen to the article to check your ideas.**

3 **Read the article again and mark the sentences T (true), F (false) or DS (doesn't say). Then correct the false sentences.**

1 Coolest Projects International is a great opportunity to meet children from all over the world. ☐
2 Over the years, fewer people have attended Coolest Projects International. ☐
3 James Whelton was brilliant at Maths at school. ☐
4 James Whelton became famous after he hacked his iPod Nano. ☐
5 Bill worked with James's father and agreed to help James. ☐
6 Teachers are paid a lot of money to run CoderDojo clubs. ☐
7 Children are free to invent and design whatever they like. ☐
8 The Romanian students' project aimed to teach children to eat more healthily. ☐

4 SPEAKING **Work in pairs and discuss the questions.**

1 Is there a CoderDojo in your town or in your country?
2 Do you think they are a good idea? Why (not)?
3 Are there any similar clubs in your area?
4 What kind of community club would you set up in your area?

GRAMMAR
Linkers of contrast

Grammar video ▶16

5 Look at these sentences about the article on page 60. Then complete the rule.

1 The children are very young. **Nevertheless**, they invent projects with a huge social impact.
2 **Although** James was no good at academic subjects at school, he was good at programming.
3 **In spite of** their young age, the kids design some amazing projects.
4 James set up the club himself **even though** he was just a student.
5 **However** young you are, you can still learn to code.
6 **Despite** having no set curriculum, students learn how to code.

RULE: To contrast ideas and facts, we use these linking words: *although, even though, however, despite, in spite of* and *nevertheless.*

7 *Despite* and ________________ are followed by a noun phrase or a gerund. They can be used at the beginning or in the middle of a sentence.
8 *Although* and ________________ are followed by a full clause. They can be used at the beginning or in the middle of a sentence.
9 *However* and ________________ introduce the contrasting idea and come at the beginning of a new sentence. They are followed by a comma.

6 Rewrite the sentences using the words in brackets.

0 I didn't know anyone at the party, but I still had a good time. (in spite of)
In spite of not knowing anyone at the party, I still had a good time.
1 I studied hard for the test. I failed it. (despite)
2 He doesn't earn a lot of money. He gives a lot of it to charity. (However)
3 I'd seen the film before. I still really enjoyed it. (although)
4 I started to eat less. I didn't lose any weight. (in spite of)
5 It wasn't very warm. We had a good time at the beach. (Nevertheless)
6 I don't speak a word of Chinese. I understood what he said. (even though)

7 Rewrite these sentences using words from the rule box.

1 I felt really tired. I stayed up till midnight to celebrate the New Year.
2 I didn't sleep well the night before the test, so I was really tired. I still got a good score.
3 He doesn't like football. He plays it with his children because they enjoy it.

→ workbook page 55

THINK values
Doing good

8 Work in groups of four. You are going to think of a project that will be good for your community or your school. Use the points below to help you organise your ideas.

1 **Decide on a project**
What does your community or school need?
How will it be good for your community or school?
2 **Plan the details of the project**
What do you need? (a meeting space, computers, a garden, etc.)
Who can help you to set it up?
3 **Think of a famous person to get involved**
Why this person?
What do you want them to do?
4 **Extras**
What other things can you do to make the project a success (write a blog about it, invite a local newspaper to write about it, hold a competition, etc.)?

9 SPEAKING **Present your ideas to the class. Each person in your group should talk about one of the points above.**

10 SPEAKING **As a class, vote on the projects with the most potential. Could you actually do these projects?**

Literature

1 **Look at the pictures and read the introduction to the extract. What do you think Mr Laurence sent Beth as a gift?**

2 6.06 **Read and listen to the extract to check your ideas.**

Little Women by Louisa May Alcott

Little Women follows the lives of the four March sisters, Jo, Beth, Meg and Amy, who grew up during and after the American Civil War (1861–1865). Mr Laurence, a wealthy old gentleman who lives next door to the family, is especially fond of Beth, as she reminds him of his little granddaughter. In this extract, Mr Laurence has sent Beth a gift and the sisters and Hannah, their only servant, are all very excited.

Beth hurried on in a flutter of suspense. At the door her sisters seized and bore her to the parlor in a triumphal procession, all pointing and all saying at once, "Look there! Look there!" Beth did look, and turned pale with delight and surprise, for there stood a little cabinet piano, with a letter lying on the glossy lid, directed like a sign board to "Miss Elizabeth March."

"For me?" gasped Beth, holding onto Jo and feeling as if she should tumble down, it was such an overwhelming thing altogether.

"Yes, all for you, my precious! Isn't it splendid of him? Don't you think he's the dearest old man in the world? Here's the key in the letter. We didn't open it, but we are dying to know what he says," cried Jo, hugging her sister and offering the note.

"You read it! I can't, I feel so queer! Oh, it is too lovely!" and Beth hid her face in Jo's apron, quite upset by her present.

Jo opened the paper and began to laugh, for the first words she saw were …

"Miss March:

"Dear Madam--"

"How nice it sounds! I wish someone would write to me so!" said Amy, who thought the old-fashioned address very elegant.

"I have had many pairs of slippers in my life, but I never had any that suited me so well as yours," continues Jo. "Heartsease is my favorite flower, and these will always remind me of the gentle giver. I like to pay my debts, so I know you will allow 'the old gentleman' to send you something which once belonged to the little granddaughter he lost. With hearty thanks and best wishes, I remain 'Your grateful friend and humble servant, JAMES LAURENCE'"

"There, Beth, that's an honor to be proud of, I'm sure! Laurie told me how fond Mr. Laurence used to be of the child who died, and how he kept all her little things carefully. Just think, he's given you her piano. That comes of having big blue eyes and loving music," said Jo, trying to soothe Beth, who trembled and looked more excited than she had ever been before.

"See the cunning brackets to hold candles, and the nice green silk, puckered up, with a gold rose in the middle, and the pretty rack and stool, all complete," added Meg, opening the instrument and displaying its beauties.

"'Your humble servant, James Laurence'. Only think of his writing that to you. I'll tell the girls. They'll think it's splendid," said Amy, much impressed by the note.

"Try it, honey. Let's hear the sound of the baby pianny," said Hannah, who always took a share in the family joys and sorrows.

So Beth tried it, and everyone pronounced it the most remarkable piano ever heard. It had evidently been newly tuned and put in apple-pie order, but, perfect as it was, I think the real charm lay in the happiest of all happy faces which leaned over it.

3 Read the extract again and answer the questions.

1 What has arrived and caused such excitement?
2 What do the sisters all want to know?
3 Whose piano was it?
4 What does Amy like about the letter?
5 What does the writer say was the best thing about receiving the piano?

4 VOCABULARY Match the highlighted words in the extract with the definitions.

1 clever
2 being modest, and not thinking of oneself as important or better than others
3 very great or very large
4 gently calm somebody
5 feeling of excitement over what may happen next
6 a perfect state
7 really want to, urgently want to
8 shiny, beautifully polished

5 SPEAKING Work in pairs and discuss the questions.

1 Jo and Beth are sisters. What do you learn about their relationship in the extract?
2 What do you learn about Beth's character in this extract?

WRITING
An essay

1 INPUT Read the essay quickly. Does the author agree or disagree with the essay title? Why?

Social media is the best way to keep in touch with friends

A These days social media is a huge part of almost everyone's life. Furthermore, it's often the quickest and easiest way to keep in touch with old friends. Therefore, it's no surprise that more and more people are using social media to keep in touch.

B Social media is a great way to stay in touch with a friend who has moved away to another town or another country. In the past, it was more difficult to stay in touch. As a consequence, after your friend left, you probably would not see them for months or even years. These days you can see them regularly online. A Skype, FaceTime or WhatsApp video call is almost the same as being in the room with your friend.

C In the past, people spoke to each other on the phone, but nowadays, people prefer to communicate with friends via text messages and emails. However, despite this being a quick and easy way to communicate, there is a negative side to it. It is easier to write mean and hurtful things to someone than it is to say them to someone face to face. As a result, teenagers may be more vulnerable to being bullied nowadays.

D Nevertheless, I still believe that social media is a fantastic way to keep in touch with old friends and even to make new friends. We just need to be careful how we use it.

2 ANALYSE Match paragraphs A–D of the essay with functions 1–4.

1 argument supporting the idea ☐
2 the writer's final opinion ☐
3 argument against the idea ☐
4 introduction ☐

3 Complete the sentences with the missing linkers. Then read the essay to check.

1 ____________, after your friend left, you probably would not see them for months or even years.
2 ____________, teenagers may be more vulnerable to being bullied nowadays.
3 ____________, I still believe that social media is a fantastic way to keep in touch with old friends and even to make new friends.
4 ____________, it's often the quickest and easiest way of keeping in touch with old friends.
5 ____________, it's no surprise that more and more people are using social media to keep in touch.
6 ____________, despite this being a quick and easy way to communicate, there is a negative side to it.

4 PLAN You're going to write your own essay with the following title. Make notes for each paragraph.

Social media brings people together

Introduction: ____________
For: ____________
Against: ____________
My conclusion: ____________

5 PRODUCE Write your essay using your notes from Exercise 4 (200–250 words).

READING AND USE OF ENGLISH

Part 7: Multiple matching

→ workbook page 53

1 You are going to read an article in which four teenagers talk about how they met their best friend. For questions 1–10, choose from the teenagers (A–D). The teenagers may be chosen more than once.

Which teenager

1 feels that they met their best friend at the perfect time? ☐
2 has changed their attitudes to best friends several times? ☐
3 has known their best friend for most of their life? ☐
4 felt an instant connection with their best friend? ☐
5 thinks that having a small number of very close friends is a positive thing? ☐
6 gets on with their best friend because they can discuss topics he doesn't talk about with his other friends? ☐
7 feels that their best friend made forming relationships with other children at school easier? ☐
8 thinks that distance helps keep a relationship healthy? ☐
9 likes having a best friend who is a different gender? ☐
10 thinks it's a good thing that their best friend doesn't know their other friends? ☐

A Dom

My best friend is Liam and I've only known him for about three months. I met Liam at a youth club and I knew immediately that he was going to be a great friend. We share exactly the same sense of humour. We like the same bands. I'm quite interested in politics and he shares exactly the same concerns as I do. It was great to finally be able to talk about something other than football and girls. Don't get me wrong, I still like talking about those things, but it's good to have a change. Also, because Liam doesn't go to the same school as me, it means that we don't waste time talking about other people.

B Gianna

I've had a lot of best friends. I remember when I was a kid, I'd have a new best friend every week. Then, when I was a bit older, I thought it was silly to have one best friend and just tried to have as many friends as I could. Recently, though, I have realised that although it's good to have lots of friends, it's even better to have one or two extra special ones that you know will always be there for you no matter what. I guess at the moment Chloe would be that friend. I really haven't known her very long, probably about a year at the most. She was the new kid in school and at first, I wasn't very friendly to her at all, probably because I already had my gang of friends. But she was in lots of my classes and I started to get to know her better and realised she was really cool.

C Anna

I still remember the first time I met Robin. I must have been about ten or eleven. I was at school when the teacher introduced him as the new student and told him to sit next to me. We were a bit shy at first, but eventually we started talking, and we've hardly stopped since. Mum says I didn't have a lot of friends at that age and I found it difficult to get on with the other kids. She says that Robin helped me find the confidence I needed to make new friends. If I hadn't met him at that point, I think I would have been quite lonely. Now we're at secondary school and we still spend lots of time together. Of course, some people think it's strange that I'm best friends with a boy, but it works for me and feels completely normal – and anyway, I tend to hang out with the girls at school and I meet up with him after school or at the weekend.

D Colin

I've known my best friend Tom since I was two. Of course, I don't remember him from then, but we met because our dads took us to the same park to play when we were toddlers. They became best friends and we grew up almost as brothers. When I was about seven, Mum and Dad moved away but they kept in touch with Tom's parents, so Tom and I would still see each other most holidays. These days, we keep in touch on Snapchat and we text each other loads. It's great having someone who knows you so well and I think the fact that we live more than 100 km apart has meant that we've become even better friends because we really value the time we have together. We don't get tired of each other because we're not living in each other's pockets.

TEST YOURSELF UNITS 5 & 6

VOCABULARY

1 Complete the sentences with the words in the list. There are four extra words.

access | backup | criticised | definition | hatchet | house | introduced
peas | protective case | shoulder | stream | sync | upgrade | zip

1 Jake is feeling really down. He could really use a ______________ to cry on.
2 My friends Emma and Nina look like two ______________ in a pod. They have the same hairstyle and dress very similarly.
3 A good way to remember new words is to learn their ______________ .
4 I know who Paul is, but I've never been ______________ to him.
5 The file was so big that I had to ______________ it to send it by email.
6 My computer runs my new graphics program very slowly. I need to ______________ it.
7 I almost lost everything when my computer crashed, but luckily, I had a ______________ of most of it.
8 The little boy and his cousin are getting on like a ______________ on fire.
9 I'm really clumsy, so the first thing I do when I get a new phone is buy a ______________ .
10 The politician was heavily ______________ for not admitting his mistake.

/10

GRAMMAR

2 Complete the sentences with the phrases in the list. There are two extra phrases.

been able | didn't need to | even though | managed to | needn't have
nowhere near as | succeeded in | wasn't allowed to

1 I've never visited the museum, ______________ I live very close to it.
2 My uncle had loads of lessons, but he never ______________ learning to drive.
3 My mum ______________ go out with her friends until she was 16.
4 The sequel is ______________ good as the first film.
5 Dax had already asked Mum about the trip, so I ______________ asked her.
6 My aunt hurt her hand last month. She hasn't ______________ to play the piano since then.

3 Find and correct the mistake in each sentence.

1 We ran as fast as we could, but we didn't manage get there in time.
2 Despite he earns a good salary, Mario says he never has enough money.
3 Nicole's parents weren't as strict with her brother than they were with her.
4 Nevertheless George's French isn't great, he understood a lot of the film.
5 It is very kind of you, but you don't need pick me up at my house. I can walk to the restaurant.
6 James always does well in tests, although never studying.

/12

FUNCTIONAL LANGUAGE

4 Choose the correct options.

1 A I think Selena Gomez's latest album is *far and away* / *miles* the best album she's ever released.
B I agree. It's *lot* / *even* better than her second album.
2 A I *must* / *need* go home now – I still have homework to finish for tomorrow.
B No, don't be silly! You *mustn't* / *don't need to* do it for tomorrow – it's a holiday.
3 A Do your parents *let* / *allow* you stay out as late as you want?
B Yes, but only at the weekends and I *have* / *must* to tell them what time I'll be home.
4 A I love this game – it's *easily* / *even* the best game I've ever played.
B No way! *Prince of Shadows* is a *whole* / *good* lot better than this.

/8

MY SCORE /30

22–30 | 10–21 | 0–9

7 ROSE-TINTED GLASSES

Get THINKING

Watch the video and think: is it important to look at things from different angles?

OBJECTIVES

FUNCTIONS: cheering someone up

GRAMMAR: ways of referring to the future (review); future continuous (review); future perfect (review)

VOCABULARY: phrases to talk about the future: *about to, off to, on the point of, due to*; feelings about future events

A

B

C

READING

1 **Look at the photos. What do they mean to you? Can you relate them to any real-life situations?**

2 SPEAKING **Read statements A and B. Discuss them in pairs. Then say who is more like you: the person who wrote statement A, or the one who wrote B.**

A My best friend has moved to another country. I'll never get over it. I won't find anybody that I like as much as her, so I won't even try to find a new friend. Imagine I finally find someone, and then she moved away, too!

B My best friend has moved to another country. That's great for her. I'm definitely going to stay in touch and I'm looking forward to hearing stories of her new life. And who knows, one day I might even be able to visit her.

3 **Read the blog quickly and answer the questions.**

1 What are the four things the husband didn't like about the past year?
2 Is the wife an optimist or a pessimist?

4 7.01 **Read and listen to the blog again. Mark the statements T (true) or F (false). Then correct the false statements.**

1 The main reason the blogger wrote this post is to share an exciting story. ☐
2 The man had to stop working last year. ☐
3 The couple's son died in a car accident. ☐
4 The car was very badly damaged in the accident. ☐
5 The woman says her husband will still have some kidney pain. ☐
6 Their son wants to study to become a doctor. ☐
7 The blogger thinks we can't control how we react to events. ☐
8 The blogger is looking forward to spending time with her brother on holiday. ☐

5 SPEAKING **Work in pairs and discuss the questions.**

1 Do you agree with the woman's opinion about what happened during the year? Or with the man's opinion?
2 Do you think a story like this could change people's attitudes? Say why (not).

My takes on life, the universe AND EVERYTHING

Take #21: It depends on how you look at it

Hi again! My take today is about a choice we have: the choice to look at things from a positive point of view, or a negative one. How we see things matters – it affects our well-being. And here's a story I found recently that illustrates my point.

It was New Year's Eve, and a couple were about to go out to celebrate. They were on the point of leaving when the man said to his wife, 'This year finishes in a few hours and I'm glad. It's been a terrible year.'

His wife asked him, 'Why do you say that last year was terrible? I don't understand!' The man was very surprised and replied, 'You don't understand? Think about what happened last year. First of all, I had an operation to remove my kidney and now I've only got one kidney and I was in bed for weeks. Remember? And then last month, I turned 65 and I was told I had to leave my job at the newspaper, to make room for someone younger. Huh! I loved that job and didn't want to retire. What am I going to do now? And then there was our son's accident! You surely haven't forgotten that, have you? Three weeks in hospital, and that meant he couldn't take his exams to get into medical school. And we had to buy a new car. Terrible year! I'm so happy it's over.'

His wife didn't say much – she went out of the room, but a few minutes later, she came back in and said, 'OK I heard what you said, but this is how I see things. Your kidney had been bothering you for years and now you won't have that pain ever again. Now that you don't have to go to work every day, you can spend more time in the garden and make it beautiful, the way you've always wanted. And yes, the car was destroyed, but our son came out alive. And now he's got more time to study, so he'll do even better in his exams next year. So, I think it was a good year. But anyway, it's gone and the new one is due to start in a few hours – it'll be another good year if we make it one.'

So there you are. We can't control the things that happen to us, or to other people, but we can control how we look at them. You can take a pessimistic attitude, or an optimistic one – it's up to you. Some things are difficult to deal with. For example, I'm seeing the dentist this afternoon, which I'm not looking forward to, but then I think about my granddad and his awful teeth and I think, 'Going to the dentist now means I probably won't have problems in the future.' And if it hurts a little? Well, nothing's forever, right?

OK, I won't be here next week, we're off on our annual family holiday. Now, how can I find a way to think positively about two weeks with my brother around all the time? I'll think of something!

Train to TH!NK

Learning to see things from a different perspective

How we see a situation influences how we feel about it and how we behave in it. Learning to look at things from a more optimistic perspective can have a positive influence on the outcome of a situation.

6 SPEAKING **Read what these people have experienced when trying to look at things from a different perspective. In pairs, discuss what and who helped them change their attitude.**

For a long time, I used to worry about everything all the time. I even used to worry about not finding anything to worry about. Then we had this discussion in class, and one of my teachers told us about this saying that I'll never forget. It may sound ridiculous, but it really helped me change my attitude. It basically says, 'For every problem under the sun, there is either a solution or there is none. If there is one, think till you find it. If there is none, then never mind it.'

I never used to believe in myself. I always thought everybody else was better than me. One day, I went out with a group of friends and we met this guy who seemed quite nice. But then I noticed that he was starting to make fun of the things I said. I became quiet and started to feel bad about myself. When I spoke to my best friend afterwards, she just said, 'So what? That guy's strange, but that's him, not you.' So I decided to ignore the guy and he soon stopped making fun of me. More importantly, I felt better about myself.

7 SPEAKING **Work in pairs and discuss any difficult situations where you could usefully apply either of the two perspectives above.**

GRAMMAR
Ways of referring to the future (review)

1 Look at the sentences from the blog. Then complete the rule with *be going to*, *will*, *the present continuous* or *the present simple*.

1 What am I going to do now?
2 I'm seeing the dentist this afternoon.
3 It'll be another good year if we make it one.
4 I probably won't have problems in the future.
5 This year finishes in a few hours.
6 I'll think of something.
7 He'll do even better in his exams next year.

RULE: We use:
8 ______________________ to talk about future facts.
9 ______________________ to talk about events that are part of a timetable or schedule.
10 ______________________ to make evidence-based predictions.
11 ______________________ to make predictions based on thoughts and opinions.
12 ______________________ to talk about plans and intentions.
13 ______________________ to refer to definite arrangements.
14 ______________________ to refer to spontaneous decisions and offers.

2 Complete the sentences using the most appropriate form of the verbs in brackets. Sometimes more than one form is possible.

1 My dad ______________________ on the eight o'clock flight from Mexico City tomorrow. (arrive)
2 Careful! You've filled that glass too full. You ______________________ it. (spill)
3 I think it ______________________ probably a lot this weekend. It's that time of year. (rain)
4 We ______________________ friends on Saturday afternoon. (see)
5 I'm sorry, I have to finish now. The film ______________________ in two minutes. (start)
6 When I get paid, I ______________________ myself a new camera. (buy)
7 Today's lunch break ______________________ five minutes shorter than usual. (be)

→ workbook page 64

VOCABULARY
Phrases to talk about the future: *about to, off to, on the point of, due to*

3 All of these sentences refer to the future. Which sentence talks about:

a future travel plans?
b the very immediate future (x2)?
c something that's expected to happen at a particular point in the future?

1 They were about to go out and celebrate.
2 We're off on our annual family holiday.
3 They were on the point of leaving.
4 The new year is due to start in a few hours.

Look
be about to / be due to + infinitive
be off to + infinitive / noun
be on the point of + verb + *-ing*

4 Choose the correct options.

1 Although this is a serious situation, Jennifer looks as if she's *about to / off to* start laughing.
2 I'm *off to / about to* the supermarket in five minutes. Do you want anything?
3 Careful! You're *off to / about to* knock the glass over.
4 My friends are *off to / about to* get a big surprise!
5 They're *off to / on the point of* France on holiday next month.
6 It's 2–0, there's only one minute left – wow, we're *on the point of / about to* winning the match!
7 Their plane is *due to / about to* arrive at three o'clock this afternoon.

→ workbook page 66

LISTENING

5 7.02 Listen to the podcast *Silver Linings* and answer the questions.

1 Complete the phrase: 'Every ______________________ has a silver lining'.
2 Explain this phrase in your own words.

6 7.02 Listen again and note down Paul's and Nadia's answers for each round.

Round 1		Round 2	
Paul:	__________	Paul:	__________
Nadia:	__________	Nadia:	__________

7 SPEAKING Work in pairs. Who would you give the points to in each situation (Nadia or Paul) and why?

GRAMMAR

Grammar video ▶18

Future continuous (review)

8 Look at these sentences from the podcast. Then choose the correct option in the rule and complete the gaps with *be* and *-ing*.

1 Every day, **I'll be writing** the novel that's going to make me rich and famous.

2 After that **I'll be sleeping** in a comfy bed.

> **RULE:** To talk about an action that will be in progress [3]*after / around* a specific future time, we use the future continuous: *will* + [4]__________ + the [5]__________ form of the verb.

9 Complete the conversation with the future simple or future continuous form of the verb in brackets.

Mei This time tomorrow, my dad and I [1]__________ (sit) on a train.

Paula Really? Where are you going? Anywhere nice?

Mei Yes. Dad's taking me to London with him on Saturday.

Paula Wow!

Mei Tomorrow morning we [2]__________ (walk) around the city doing a bit of shopping.

Paula Great! I [3]__________ (phone) you on Saturday afternoon.

Mei Well, that's not really a good time. On Saturday afternoon we [4]__________ (watch) the football match. Chelsea against Arsenal. I can't wait! You know how much I like football.

Paula And you [5]__________ (come) home happy and relaxed. Lucky you.

Mei Well, I hope so. It's an important game for Chelsea.

Paula It all sounds wonderful. So, what time's your train tomorrow?

Mei 8 o'clock.

Paula Alright. At 8.30, I [6]__________ (think) of you.

Mei And I [7]__________ (put) some photos from our weekend on Instagram – if I remember.

Future perfect (review)

10 Look at the example sentences and complete the rule with *have, past participle* and *will*.

1 … after three weeks of that, you'll have annoyed your entire family.

2 In a few years' time, I'll have married an Italian.

> **RULE:** To talk about an action that will finish at some time between now and a specified time in the future, we use the future perfect. We often use it with the preposition *by* + [3]__________ + [4]__________ + [5]__________ .

11 Choose the correct verb forms.

1 By the time Mum comes back from work, I will *be finishing / have finished* my homework.

2 By 2050, psychologists will *be finding / have found* ways to help pessimists feel more optimistic.

3 Don't call after 10 pm. I will *be sleeping / have slept*.

4 This time tomorrow morning I will *be flying / have flown* to Singapore. We land in the afternoon.

5 When I leave school, I will *be spending / have spent* six years there.

6 You can find Miss Green in classroom 3. She will *be teaching / have taught* there until midday.

7 We're going to watch films all day on Saturday. By the end of the day, we will *be watching / have watched* more than five films!

8 The band will *be touring / have toured* for six months later this year to promote their new album.

→ workbook page 65

SPEAKING

12 Work in groups of four and play *Silver Linings*. Read the situations and think of optimistic solutions. Make notes.

Student A: Your best friend completely forgets your birthday.

Student B: Someone pours orange juice over your new T-shirt.

Student C: You fail your History exam.

Student D: Your country doesn't qualify for the football World Cup.

13 Take turns to talk about the 'silver linings' in your situations. Give a point for each correct use of the future continuous or the future perfect. Award five points for the most imaginative answer.

QUOTATIONS FOR WORRIERS

'You'll never find a RAINBOW if you look down!'

Who said that? No, it wasn't me. It was Charlie Chaplin and I love it. You should know that I wasn't exactly born an optimist myself. I was actually quite a worrier until I discovered the power of inspirational quotes. Try me. Send me a worry, and I'll send you a quote. For free. If you like the quote, please let me know. Positive messages help me, too, and so far, all the feedback has been positive!

A SHALL I STAY OR SHALL I GO?

Hi, I don't know what to do. I've got an aunt and uncle in the US, and they've invited me to go there for a month or so. Sounds cool, doesn't it? But I'm worried there won't be anyone my age to hang out with. They live in a smallish sort of town, and they haven't got any kids themselves. It may sound weird, but I feel that whatever I decide, I'll probably regret it later! Can you help? I hope so.

B DRUMMER BOY

I got this drum kit for my 16th birthday. There's a band at my school. They're great, but their drummer, Luca, is leaving at the end of the school year – his family is moving to another town. The band have asked me if I want to audition and Luca has offered to teach me. But I'm not sure I'll be good enough. I don't think I should get my hopes up. I'd be so disappointed if I didn't get in.

1 ☐ Hmm. Yes, I understand that's not an easy situation. But I don't think that means you should just sit around complaining that everything's gloomy. Maybe what Anne Frank said will help you to be more optimistic: 'How wonderful it is that nobody needs to wait a single moment before starting to improve the world.'

2 ☐ Look, this is for you, and it's by Mahatma Gandhi. I'll say no more. It's all in the quote. 'Man often becomes what he believes himself to be. If I keep on saying to myself that I cannot do a certain thing, it is possible that I may end by really becoming incapable of doing it. On the contrary, if I have the belief that I can do it, I shall surely acquire the capacity to do it even if I may not have it at the beginning.'

3 ☐ My quote for you is by Winston Churchill. 'A pessimist sees the difficulty in every opportunity; an optimist sees the opportunity in every difficulty.' Even if you are right, there are probably about a million things you can do there that you can't do at home! So I'd say, go. And remember the rainbow!

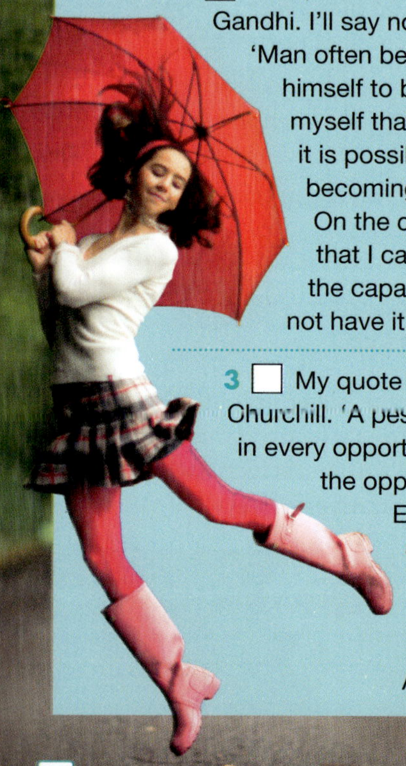

READING

1 **Read this webpage quickly. Who is it for? What are the two worries mentioned by the people who've posted on the website?**

2 7.03 **Read and listen to the webpage again. Match the answers with the worries. There is one extra quote.**

3 **Read the webpage again and answer the questions.**

1 What does the writer have in common with the two worriers?
2 What is the difference between the writer and the two worriers?
3 Are the two worriers equally pessimistic? Why (not)?
4 What is the writer referring to in the third answer by saying, 'And remember the rainbow!'?

4 SPEAKING **Work in pairs and discuss the questions.**

1 What kind of person is the owner of this website? Would you like to get to know them? Why (not)?
2 Do you think quotations can cheer you up when you're down?
3 How would you react if you were in the situation of one of the two worriers?
4 Look at the extra quote. What kind of problem could this quote be an answer to?
5 Which of the three quotes do you like most? Why?

VOCABULARY
Feelings about future events

5 SPEAKING Work in pairs. Make a list of five situations or events which can make you feel worried.

6 Read the following extracts from *Quotations for worriers*. What situation or event do you think each extract refers to?

A It's a big game and **I'm feeling quite apprehensive**. If we win, we'll be top of the league. I'm excited, but they're a good team and in the last two games we were only so-so. So **I'm unsure about** our chances.

B **I've got a really good feeling about** this. **I'm really looking forward to** it and **I feel quite positive about** it. If I'm honest, I'll probably be old enough to be the other students' mother, but so what? It's something I really want to do. Any suggestions for how I can bridge the age gap with my new classmates?

C **I've just got a bad feeling about** this. I'm sure I'm going to fail. I haven't done any revision and **I just don't know where to start** … **It's a nightmare – I'm really worried** about it.

D **I'm dreading** this, but I'm not sure why **I'm getting so worked up**. I've seen him loads of times before and he's really good, but I've just got a bad feeling about it this time. I think I need to have one of my teeth taken out.

7 Look at the phrases in bold and use them to complete each list. If needed, use a dictionary to help you with meaning.

expressing optimism	expressing pessimism / worry
I'm really looking forward to …	*I'm dreading …*

8 Match the phrases from Exercise 7 with the events you listed in Exercise 5 in which you might use them.

→ workbook page 66

WordWise: Expressions with *so*

9 Look at these sentences from the unit so far. Complete them with phrases from the list.

I hope so | or so | so far
so not | so-so | so what

1 A Can you help?
B ______________________ .
2 In the last two games we were only ______________________ .
3 ______________________ , all the feedback's been positive!
4 That will feel a bit odd, but ______________________ ?
5 I'm ______________________ looking forward to this.
6 They've invited me to go there for a month ______________________ .

10 Complete the sentences with the expressions from Exercise 9.

1 A Andrew isn't going to like this.
B ______________________ ? I'm not worried about Andrew.
2 I'd hoped the film would be really good, but it was only ______________________ .
3 I'm going to read a different book. I'm ______________________ enjoying this one.
4 My mum's gone to Rome for a week ______________________ , to work.
5 I'm taking guitar lessons, and ______________________ I'm really enjoying them.
6 A Do you think we're going to have fun at the beach?
B ______________________ , I really need some relaxation.

→ workbook page 66

WRITING
A short story

11 You are going to write a story (200–250 words) which finishes with the words, 'Every cloud has a silver lining.'

Think of:
- an unfortunate incident
- an unexpected positive outcome
- how it changed the main character's life.

DEVELOPING SPEAKING

1 7.04 **Look at the photo. What do you think Matt is doing? Read and listen to check.**

Zoe: Hey, Matt. What's up? You look terrible.
Matt: Hi, Zoe. Well, I had an audition this afternoon – you know, for a part in a play. It was awful.
Zoe: Come on, Matt, cheer up! I'm sure it wasn't that bad.
Matt: Oh, it was! It really was. <u>For a start</u> I was late, then I read the wrong lines, then I started coughing. I <u>made a real fool of myself</u>! Am I a fool? Am I a terrible actor?
Zoe: Well, to be honest it sounds like you might have prepared better. But don't let it get you down. One bad audition doesn't mean you haven't got talent.
Matt: I guess. But I really wanted that part. I need parts to have a better chance of getting into drama school.
Zoe: Well, let's look on the bright side. There'll be more auditions, won't there?
Matt: Yes, sure. In fact, I <u>put my name down</u> for another audition next week, but I don't think I want to go.
Zoe: No, Matt. Go for it. You don't have anything to lose.
Matt: I just don't want to <u>get my hopes up</u> for nothing.
Zoe: <u>Fair enough</u>. Getting turned down isn't easy. But you've got to hang in there!
Matt: I know. Thanks, Zoe. You always manage to cheer me up, I really appreciate it. <u>Anyway</u>, how was your day?
Zoe: Well, nothing special, but it was better than yours, I think! Come on, let's get an ice cream!

2 7.04 **Read and listen to the dialogue again and answer the questions.**

1 What went wrong at Matt's audition?
2 Why is Matt thinking of not doing the audition next week?
3 How does Zoe encourage Matt?

3 SPEAKING **Discuss the statements in pairs. Do you agree with them?**

1 One bad [audition/day/exam/game] doesn't mean you haven't got talent.
2 Matt should 'hang in there'.

Phrases for fluency

4 **Find the <u>underlined</u> expressions in the dialogue and use them to complete the conversations.**

1 A Well, there are lots of reasons I don't want to go there. It's very expensive, ____________________ .
B ____________________ . We'll have to think of another place to go, then.
2 A There's a singing competition at school next month. I thought I might ____________________ .
B Well, don't ____________________ . Sophie Kenny's bound to win it.
3 A So have you decided to try out for the team?
B No, I decided not to. I'm not good enough and I'd only ____________________ .
A That's a shame and I'm sure that wouldn't happen.
B ____________________ , even if I did get in, they play on Saturday mornings and I like to have a lie-in on Saturdays.

5 SPEAKING **Work in pairs. One of you is Zoe, the other is Matt. Imagine it is five years later and you meet again. Act out two scenarios.**

1 Matt has taken his acting career further.
2 Matt has given up acting.

FUNCTIONS
Cheering someone up

KEY LANGUAGE

Cheer up!	Hang in there!
Don't let it get you down.	Look on the bright side.
There's light at the end of the tunnel.	

6 **Complete the sentences with phrases from the Key Language box.**

1 ____________________ up! Things will seem better after a good night's sleep.
2 ____________________ there. Your exams will be over soon.
3 Don't let ____________________ . It's not the end of the world.
4 I can see that losing the match is really bothering you, but try to look ____________________ side – it's early in the season.
5 I know this year of high school can be really difficult, but there is ____________________ tunnel!

7 SPEAKING **Work in pairs. Think of situations in which someone would need cheering up. Write short dialogues using the language from the Key Language box. Then act them out.**

PRONUNCIATION
Intonation: encouraging someone
Go to page 121.

LIFE COMPETENCIES

It's important to be honest with your friends, but sometimes being too sincere can cause upset or offence. In such situations we need to use tact and show sensitivity to how others may be feeling.

1 ▶ 19 **Watch the vlog. What three presents did Chloe get from her aunt?**

2 ▶ 19 **Watch the vlog again and make notes about:**

a Chloe's truthful thoughts
b things she could say to be tactful.

3 SPEAKING **Work in pairs. Think of three more things Chloe could have said to be tactful.**

4 SPEAKING **Read the situation and the responses. Work in pairs and discuss which response is the most tactful.**

A friend has bought a new outfit for the school disco, and wants your opinion on it. The outfit was expensive and they think they look great in it. However, you don't agree. You think the clothes are out of fashion and don't suit your friend at all. What do you say?

A Whatever you do, don't wear them. They're so unfashionable and you look terrible in them.
B You look great in them. You'll be a big success.
C If I'm honest, I think blue is a better colour for you.

5 **Read the situation. In pairs, think of a reply that is tactful. Then compare your ideas with another pair.**

1

You are in a team of four, working on an important project for school. While three of you are working your hardest to get the best result possible, the other member is not doing their fair share of the work. You want to say something before it's too late, but what?

2

You're in a band with a couple of friends from school. You've been together for about a year and are now quite good. You've played several shows and are getting more popular. Your best friend wants to be part of the action and has asked if he could join the band as a singer. You know that his voice isn't very good. What do you say?

Me and my world

6 **Think of a time when you found yourself in an awkward situation (e.g. someone turned up at a party that they hadn't been invited to) and make notes.**

- Who did it involve?
- What did they want?
- Why was it awkward?
- Would you do things differently if it happened again?

7 SPEAKING **Work in pairs and tell your partner about the situation. Then discuss these questions below.**

1 Is it sometimes better to just be honest? Can you think of an example?
2 Who's the most direct person you know? What sort of things do they say?
3 Do you consider yourself to be tactful? Give examples.

TIPS FOR BEING TACTFUL

- Before giving negative feedback, think about how you would react if someone gave you similar news.
- It's always a good idea to try and focus on something positive first – this will make it easier to deliver the negative comments afterwards.
- It is possible to be too tactful. Make sure your message isn't lost in too much tact.

8 LIST IT!

OBJECTIVES

FUNCTIONS: saying 'yes' and adding conditions

GRAMMAR: conditionals (review); mixed conditionals

VOCABULARY: phrasal verbs (2); alternatives to *if*: *suppose, provided, as long as, otherwise, unless*

Get THINKING

Watch the video and think: what kinds of lists do you make?

A

C

B

D
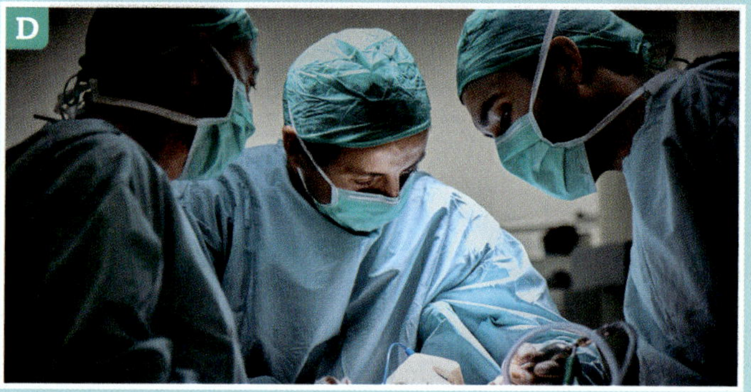

READING

1 SPEAKING **Look at the photos. Work in pairs and think about the things on the list below. Then compare your ideas with other people in the class.**

1 three ways in which the jobs are different
2 three things the jobs have in common
3 something that connects *all* of them

2 **Read the book review quickly. What does Atul Gawande recommend using to ensure procedures are followed?**

3 8.01 **Read and listen to the review. Match the paragraphs with the titles. There is one extra title.**

A Lives can be saved ☐
B It's not just for the medical profession ☐
C Mistakes don't really matter ☐
D Holes in the system ☐
E Not everyone agrees ☐
F A book for everyone ☐

4 **Read the article again and answer the questions.**

1 What surprised the doctor who went into the operating theatre?
2 What was the result of an experiment in an important American hospital?
3 What examples does Gawande give of what could happen if engineers and pilots didn't follow checklists?
4 How did many of the doctors react to the idea of using checklists? Why do you think they reacted this way?
5 Why does the writer of the review recommend the book?

5 SPEAKING **Work in pairs and discuss the questions.**

1 Can you think of any other jobs where checklists should be compulsory?
2 Have you ever made any checklists for yourself? What for? Were they useful?
3 Do you agree with the last sentence in the review? Why (not)?

THE CHECKLIST MANIFESTO BY ATUL GAWANDE

1 A doctor in a large hospital walked into an operating theatre where an operation was being performed. Everything seemed to be going well, but the doctor picked up on one disturbing fact – no one was wearing a face mask. He was a little shocked – wearing a face mask is basic hospital procedure. But he didn't say anything. The operation was a success, but a few days later the patient came down with a fever. It turned out that she had a serious infection, probably because the doctors and nurses hadn't followed a simple rule. If they'd worn their masks, the patient wouldn't have been infected.

2 Someone who'd be interested in that story is Atul Gawande, who wrote a book called *The Checklist Manifesto: How to get things right*. Gawande is a doctor himself, and in his book he suggests that if surgeons run through a simple checklist before every operation, then lives will be saved. And he's got the numbers to prove it. In 2001, at an important American hospital, there was an experiment that required doctors to use a five-point checklist before they carried out specific procedures. The checklist was just a list of routine things doctors should normally do without thinking – for example, wearing rubber gloves, washing hands before and after every patient, and so on. By making sure that the checklist was followed, there were almost no infections over the 27 months of the experiment, and they reckon that around eight lives were saved. When the checklist was tried out again in hospitals in Michigan, in the US, infections went down by 66 percent.

3 In his book, Gawande looks at other professions, too, to support his argument that checklists reduce accidents and improve success rates. He points out that people like engineers and pilots use checklists all the time, and he comes up with some good examples. Just imagine that an aeroplane crashed because the pilot had failed to follow basic procedures. Suppose a skyscraper fell down because the engineers hadn't remembered to do some important calculations. There would be an immediate inquiry to look into these events. So Gawande's question is: if pilots and engineers use checklists, why don't doctors use them?

4 But when Gawande talked to doctors at eight hospitals about a checklist that he had developed, he found that a lot of them weren't very enthusiastic. Twenty percent of the doctors that Gawande talked to said that the list was too difficult to use and that it wouldn't help to save lives. But, when they were shown the statement, 'If I had surgery, I'd want the surgeon to use this list', 93 percent of the same doctors agreed with it! So it's hard to work out why they don't want to use it themselves.

5 *The Checklist Manifesto* is a really interesting and well-written book. It reminds us to do basic things to avoid problems. It's relevant for all of us, not just for doctors. We should all use checklists now and again, otherwise we'll make mistakes.

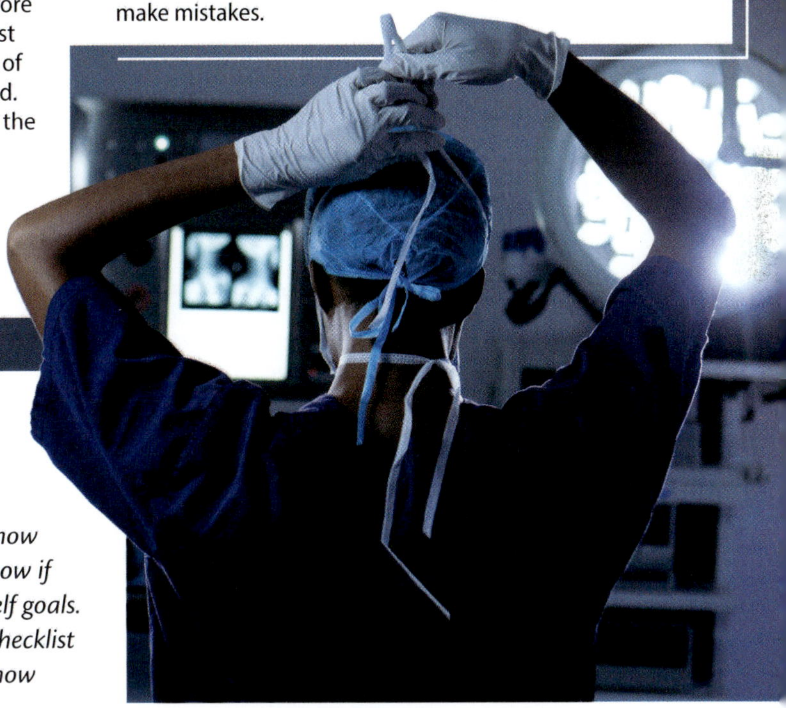

Train to TH!NK

The 'goal-setting' checklist

When you go on a journey, you wouldn't say to yourself, 'I don't know where to go to, but I'll start my journey anyway.' You will never know if your destination is where you wanted to be, if you don't set yourself goals. This is important for all of our 'journeys' in life. The 'goal-setting' checklist helps you think clearly about what it is you want to achieve and how you're going to achieve it.

6 **Max has a new project. He wants to learn to play the piano. Look at these ideas that Max has written and match them with items 1–5 in the checklist. (Some include more than one idea and some could go in more than one place on the checklist.)**

- a I'll be able to play about 20 songs. ☐
- b approach it as something to be enjoyed ☐
- c I'll feel really good about my achievement. ☐
- d learn to play the piano ☐
- e positive comments from family and friends ☐
- f a friend who will teach me ☐
- g discipline to practise daily ☐
- h lessons streamed from the internet ☐

- ☐ 1 What I want to achieve
- ☐ 2 Things I need in order to achieve this goal
- ☐ 3 How I need to act or behave in order to achieve this goal
- ☐ 4 Things that tell me I have achieved this goal
- ☐ 5 Results of achieving this goal, for myself and for others

7 SPEAKING **Think of something you want to achieve. Use the checklist to help you define your goals more clearly. Compare your ideas with a partner.**

GRAMMAR
Conditionals (review)

1 **Write the correct form of the verbs in brackets and check in the review on page 75. Then complete the table.**

1 If surgeons ____________ (run) through a simple checklist before every operation, then lives ____________ (be) saved.

2 If they ____________ (wear) their masks, the patient ____________ (not be) infected.

3 If pilots and engineers ____________ (use) checklists, why ____________ doctors ____________ (use) them?

4 If I ____________ (have) surgery, I ____________ (want) the surgeon to use this list.

RULE:

Type of conditional	Example sentence	*If* clause	Main clause
Zero	3	present simple	5 ____________
First	6 ____________	7 ____________	8 ____________
Second	9 ____________	10 ____________	*would(n't)* + infinitive
Third	11 ____________	past perfect	12 ____________

2 **Match the four sentences a doctor might say to a patient with situations a–d.**

1 If people take this medicine, they don't get headaches. ☐
2 If you take this medicine, you won't get headaches. ☐
3 If you took this medicine, you wouldn't get headaches. ☐
4 If you had taken this medicine, you wouldn't have got headaches. ☐

a The patient didn't take the medicine.
b The doctor is telling the patient a general fact about the medicine.
c The patient isn't taking the medicine, and gets headaches.
d The doctor is telling the patient about a future result of taking the medicine.

3 **Write sentences using the type of conditional specified.**

1 Reading books is a great idea. (0 conditional) If you / read books, you / learn things about life.

2 I think you should buy the book. (1st conditional) You / discover interesting things about pilots and doctors if you / read it.

3 Gawande's a doctor. (2nd conditional) If Gawande / not be a doctor, he / not understand so much about this.

4 I read this book a week or two ago. (3rd conditional) I / not find out about the importance of checklists if I / not read it.

→ workbook page 72

VOCABULARY
Phrasal verbs (2)

4 **Complete the sentences with the phrases in the list. Then check your answers in the review on page 75.**

came down with | carried out | comes up with | picked up on | points out | run through | tried out | turned out

1 The doctor ____________________ one disturbing fact.
2 The patient ____________________ a fever.
3 It ____________________ that she had a serious infection.
4 If surgeons ____________________ a simple checklist before every operation, then lives will be saved.
5 There was an experiment that required doctors to use a [...] checklist before they ____________________ specific procedures.
6 When the checklist was ____________________ again in hospitals in Michigan, US, infections went down by 66 percent.
7 Gawande ____________________ that people like engineers and pilots use checklists all the time.
8 He ____________________ some good examples.

5 SPEAKING **Work in pairs and discuss the meaning of the phrasal verbs from Exercise 4.**

6 **Use the correct form of seven of the verbs from Exercise 4 to complete the short story.**

It was two days before the school camping trip. The teacher gathered everyone in the school hall because she wanted to 1 ____________________ some things. She gave us all a list she had 2 ____________________ of things we needed. Someone 3 ____________________ that this was a bit late, but she didn't 4 ____________________ on this. She just continued talking. She was like an army general about to 5 ____________________ an important attack. She had everything planned out, every last detail. The camping trip was getting less attractive by the minute. I looked at the list. How was I going to get all these things in 48 hours? Well, it 6 ____________________ I needn't have worried. The next day, the teacher 7 ____________________ with the flu and the whole thing was called off.

→ workbook page 74

LISTENING

7 SPEAKING **Work in pairs. Look at this list. Which of these things would you be interested in doing?**

Things to do before you are 25:
- *Parachute out of a plane* ☐
- *Visit every continent* ☐
- *Write a novel* ☐
- *Meet a famous person* ☐

8 8.02 **Listen to Tom's great-grandfather giving a talk at Tom's school. Next to the items on the list above, write T (for things on Tom's bucket list) and G (for things his great-grandfather has done).**

9 8.02 **Listen again and complete Mr Hardeman's concerns in four words or less.**

1 Tom might feel ____________ if he doesn't complete his list.
2 The ideas on the list are not really Tom's, but someone ____________ .
3 If Tom focuses too much on his list he will ____________ everyday life.

10 SPEAKING **Work in pairs. Which of the concerns above do you agree with? Why?**

11 SPEAKING **Complete this bucket list for you. Then compare your list with a partner's list.**

Five things to do before finishing school:

1 ____________
2 ____________
3 ____________
4 ____________
5 ____________

GRAMMAR

Mixed conditionals

Grammar video ▶21

12 8.03 **Complete the sentences from the talk with the words or phrases in the list. Listen and check.**

had | was | would | would have

1 If I ____________ younger, I ____________ known what a bucket list was.
2 If I ____________ made a list, what ____________ be on it?

13 Look at the sentences again. Underline the second and third conditional parts in each one. Then match them to the sentences in the rule.

RULE: Sometimes we mix second and third conditional forms so that we can connect present and past actions.

- To talk about the present result of an unreal or imagined past action we use: *if* + *had* + past participle, *would ('d)* + infinitive. Sentence [1] ____________
- To talk about the past result of an unreal or hypothetical present situation or fact, we use: *if* + past simple, *would ('d) have* + past participle. Sentence [2] ____________

14 Write mixed conditional sentences to describe these situations.

0 I don't have any money. I didn't buy that phone.
If I had some money, I'd have bought that phone.
1 Anna and Dan had a big argument. They aren't talking to each other.
2 We didn't leave early. That's why we're late now.
3 I don't have a good memory. I forgot her birthday.
4 I didn't eat breakfast. Now I'm hungry.
5 He didn't pay attention. He can't do the homework.

15 Work in pairs. Use the gapped sentences. How many different mixed conditional examples can you make in five minutes?

1 If I hadn't ____________ yesterday, I wouldn't be ____________ now.
2 If I was ____________ , I would have ____________ .
3 I wouldn't have ____________ if I didn't like .
4 I would ____________ if I had ____________ at school.

→ workbook page 73

PRONUNCIATION
Weak forms with conditionals Go to page 121.

Elisa's LIST BLOG

As you know, every week I post a top ten list here that someone has sent me. Well, this week, no one has sent me anything, so I'm offering you a top ten list of … my favourite top ten lists! And here they are.

1 Ten of the world's strangest sports
Everything from extreme ironing to cheese rolling and toe wrestling. You won't see any of these sports at the Olympics.

2 Ten crazy hotels
Suppose you fancied a night in a volcano … Or how about a sandcastle or inside a giant wooden dog? There's plenty of inspiration for your next holiday here.

3 Top things you never knew your brain could do
Did you know you can learn while you're asleep? And that you can predict the future? Or know what's happening behind you without looking? Well, you can. And there's a lot more your brain can do, too.

4 Ten amazing ways that animals communicate
Elephants use their heads and tails to communicate. Honey bees dance and mushrooms have their own 'internet'. The facts will fascinate you, as long as you're interested in nature.

5 Amazing things people have found on the beach
Thousands of rubber ducks, an enormous tree, eight-foot-tall Lego men … You just never know what might turn up when you take a walk along the shoreline!

6 Ten criminals who needed to phone 999 to escape
A burglar who got stuck in a chimney. A petrol station robber who got his arm stuck in a window. A car thief who got stuck in a car. Read all about them here – unless you've got something better to do.

7 Everyday inventions from Victorian times
Cement, chocolate, flushing toilets, the sewing machine, the underground, the radio and the X-ray – all invented by the Victorians, but we couldn't live without them today.

8 Ten superhero powers you could actually learn
Fancy being a superhero? Well, here are the powers you could learn to help you on your way, provided you've got the time. Powers include super strength, speed and agility. And mind control!

9 Before they were famous
They weren't always mega-famous: before turning her hand to acting, Meghan Markle was a calligrapher (that means she wrote things in nice handwriting), Beyoncé swept hair from the floor of a salon and Brad Pitt wore a chicken costume to advertise a restaurant. Well, we've all got to start somewhere.

10 Ten amazing facts about the world around us
The amount of water in our world never changes. It just gets recycled. That means that cup of water you drank this morning might have been drunk by a dinosaur 350 million years before. And that's just the least interesting fact! Fascinating!

So, that's me done for this week. You can find these lists in my archive. Lastly – please send me a list, people, otherwise I won't have anything for next week.

READING

1 SPEAKING **Work in pairs and discuss what 'top ten' lists you have seen (or written) recently.**

2 8.06 **Read and listen to the blog. Answer the questions.**

1 Why is Elisa posting her own list this week?
2 Where can you see the complete lists?
3 What does Elisa want her readers to do?

3 **Read the blog again. Which list do each of these sentences come from? Write a number (1–10) in the boxes.**

a One man wasn't so lucky. While trying to rob a bank, the safe fell on him and crushed him to death. ☐
b Wim Hof set a world record when he buried himself in freezing ice for 72 minutes, wearing only a pair of shorts. ☐
c Everyone has heard of horse racing – but in some parts of the world people race on ostriches. ☐
d Perhaps the most remarkable of all, though, was the telephone, which changed the way people communicate with each other forever. ☐
e You can even learn to play the piano just by imagining you're playing it. ☐

4 SPEAKING **Which three lists would you like to read in full? Compare your ideas with a partner.**

5 SPEAKING **Choose one of these ideas, or use your own idea, to write a new top ten list. Then compare your lists in groups.**

- My top five most interesting …
- My top five worst …
- My top five strangest …
- My top five funniest …

THINK values

Lists

6 Tick (✓) the sentences you agree with.

1 ☐ I never waste my time reading top ten lists.
2 ☐ Top ten lists aren't meant to be taken seriously – just enjoy them!
3 ☐ Some top ten lists can be very useful.
4 ☐ People who write top ten lists must have a very high opinion of themselves.

7 SPEAKING Compare your choices in pairs.

8 Which of these top ten lists would interest you? Put a tick (✓) or a cross (✗). Add one more thing of your own that you think would make for an interesting top ten list.

- someone's favourite songs ☐
- things to do before you're 20 ☐
- ways to make money ☐
- things to do to relax and be happy ☐
- ______________________

VOCABULARY

Alternatives to *if*: *suppose, provided, as long as, otherwise, unless*

Look

To hypothesise about the present: *suppose* + past simple, *would* + infinitive

To talk about a future possibility and its results: *as long as* / *unless* + present simple, *will* + infinitive

9 Match the sentence halves.

1 **Suppose** you fancied ☐
2 The facts will fascinate you, ☐
3 Read all about them here ☐
4 Here are the powers you could learn to help you on your way, ☐
5 Please send me a list, ☐

a **provided** you've got the time.
b **as long as** you're interested in nature.
c a night in a volcano …
d **otherwise** I won't have anything for next week.
e – **unless** you've got something better to do.

10 Match the words in bold in Exercise 9 with these meanings.

1 but only if: *as long as* / ______________
2 imagine: ______________
3 if … not …: ______________
4 because if not: ______________

11 Complete with *unless*, *provided* or *otherwise*.

1 I don't mind going to the cinema alone, ______________ it's a film I really want to see.
2 I think I should go home now, ______________ my parents will be worried.
3 You'll do fine in the exam, ______________ you study enough.
4 I'll never speak to you again ______________ you say sorry right now!
5 OK, I'll tell you what happened, ______________ you promise not to tell anyone else!
6 ______________ you start to work harder, you won't pass the exam next month.

→ workbook page 74

FUNCTIONS

Saying 'yes' and adding conditions

12 SPEAKING Work in pairs. Read the sentences and discuss who is talking to whom and what they are talking about.

1 You can borrow it if you drive really carefully. (as long as)
2 Yes, you can go to the party, if you promise to be home by 11 o'clock. (provided)
3 If you don't help me, I'll get a really bad mark. (unless)
4 I'll fix it if you let me play games on it. (as long as)
5 Close the door, or it'll get cold in here. (otherwise)
6 Yes, you can practise if you don't make a lot of noise. (provided)
7 Imagine you could play the guitar – what kind of music would you play? (suppose)

13 Rewrite the sentences in Exercise 12, using the words in brackets.

14 A friend asks you these things. For each one, on what conditions would you say yes? Make notes.

1 Can I use your phone to make a call?
no international phone calls / no long phone calls
2 Will you come shopping with me?
3 Please come to the football match with me.
4 Can I borrow your jacket, please?

15 SPEAKING Use your notes from Exercise 14 to write your answers. Then work with a partner and act out the conversations for the situations.

Yes, of course – as long as / provided you don't make any long calls on it.

TH!NK

Wonders of the world

Culture

1 SPEAKING **Work in pairs and look at the photos. Discuss what you know about these places.**

2 8.07 **Read and listen to the article and answer the questions.**

1 Which wonder is the highest? 2 Which wonder is the longest?

Seven Wonders of THE NATURAL WORLD

The seven wonders of the natural world will inspire amazement from anyone who sees them. They are a constant reminder of the fragile beauty of our planet.

THE GRAND CANYON, ARIZONA, US

Around 17 million years ago, the Colorado River started to carve out its course through the Arizonian wilderness and the Grand Canyon was born. The Canyon is more than 450 km long, around 28 km at its widest point and around 1.5 km at its deepest. It is one of America's most visited natural wonders.

PARICUTIN, MICHOACÁN, MEXICO

There are many impressive volcanoes all over the world. But what makes Paricutin so special is that it was born, grew up and went extinct all in about 20 years, giving scientists a unique opportunity to study the life cycle of a volcano. Paricutin quickly grew to a height of 423 m. Then, in 1952, after 19 years of eruptions, it went quiet.

AURORA BOREALIS, AURORA AUSTRALIS

Visitors to the Earth's Polar Regions may well get to witness a spectacular display of colourful lights in the night sky. The Northern lights (Aurora Borealis) and Southern lights (Aurora Australis) are the result of particles from outer space entering into the Earth's atmosphere. The closer you are to the poles, the more vibrant the displays will be.

VICTORIA FALLS, AFRICA

They're not the tallest or widest waterfalls in the world, but if you are measuring the amount of water that falls over them each second, they are certainly the biggest. These waterfalls, found on the Zambezi River as it enters Zimbabwe from Zambia, were named by the British explorer David Livingstone, after Queen Victoria. These days the local name Mosi-oa-Tunya (the smoke that thunders) is preferred by many.

RIO DE JANEIRO HARBOUR, BRAZIL

When Portuguese sailors first sailed into Guanabara Bay on January 1st 1502, and landed on the shore, they gave it the name Rio de Janeiro (river of January) as they believed they were at the mouth of a large river. In fact, they were in a bay that stretched for almost 30 km.

THE GREAT BARRIER REEF, AUSTRALIA

More than 3,000 reefs and nearly 1,000 islands make up the Great Barrier Reef and at around 2,250 km in length, it's the only natural object on Earth that is visible from outer space. These days the reef receives special protection from the Australian government to ensure its survival.

MOUNT EVEREST, THE HIMALAYAS

Mount Everest is one of the most well-known natural features of our planet. Standing at over 8,500 metres, it is the highest mountain in the world. Since it was first conquered by Tenzing Norgay and Edmund Hilary in 1953, thousands have climbed to the summit.

3 **Read the article again and complete each sentence with one of the seven wonders.**

1 ______________________ was mistaken for being something else.
2 ______________________ can be seen in both of the Earth's hemispheres.
3 ______________________ can be seen by astronauts from the Space Station.
4 ______________________ is more than 17 million years old.
5 ______________________ was first climbed in 1953.
6 ______________________ was formed very quickly.
7 ______________________ is on the border between two countries.

4 VOCABULARY **Match the highlighted words in the article with the definitions.**

1 bright and colourful
2 way
3 the top of something
4 where sea meets land
5 delicate
6 can be seen
7 died out
8 explosions

5 SPEAKING **Work in pairs and discuss the questions.**

1 Imagine you could choose one of the seven wonders to go and see. Which one would it be and why?
2 Think of two things from your country that you could campaign to be included on a list of seven wonders of the natural world. Give reasons to support your choice.

WRITING
An essay

1 INPUT **Read Javed's essay. What can you see from the top of Mount Bromo, if the weather is good?**

A wonder of the natural world

My choice for a wonder of the natural world is Mount Bromo in Indonesia. Indonesia has many wonderful volcanoes [1]and Mount Bromo, on the eastern side of the island of Java, is [2]... most beautiful. It rises [3]up of a large plain known as 'the sea of sand'. It's just over 2,300 metres to the top of the crater, which can be reached on foot. The crater is huge and the views across it are amazing. Inside the crater, there are other smaller volcanoes, so you have the effect of having one volcano inside another. It is a popular tourist attraction and sometimes [4]there can be quite a big crowd of people there. Most people [5]spend the night before in a nearby village called Cemoro Lawang. They get up really early the next morning and make the 45-minute walk to the top in time to see the sunrise over the far side of the equator. If you are unlucky, there will be too many clouds, [6]but on a clear day it is [7]won of the most beautiful sunrises you will see anywhere in the world.

Mount Bromo is still active and occasionally erupts, so you need to be careful when visiting it. In fact, in 2004, two people [8]had been killed by rocks that were thrown into the air [9]by an eruption. However, such events are extremely rare and when there is danger of activity, the local authorities [10]... make sure that no one goes up.

2 ANALYSE **Read the essay again. Ten things are underlined. Five of the things are mistakes, the other five are correct. Find an example of:**

- a spelling mistake
- a mistake with the verb tense
- a mistake with the wrong choice of connecting word
- a mistake with a preposition
- a mistake which is a missing word

3 **Correct the mistakes in Javed's writing.**

4 **Look again at the list of kinds of mistakes in Exercise 2.**

1 Are there other kinds of mistakes that people make in writing? What are they (e.g. punctuation)?
2 Does the list in Exercise 2 show the kinds of mistakes that you have sometimes made in your writing so far using this book? If you've made other kinds of mistakes, what were they?
3 Make a checklist for yourself of 'Mistakes I should try not to make when I write in English'.

5 PLAN **You're going to write an essay entitled: 'A Wonder of the Natural World'.**

1 Choose a natural wonder in your country or somewhere else in the world.
2 Make notes about why you think this is a good choice for a modern wonder of the world.

6 PRODUCE **Write your essay (200–250 words).**

- Make sure you state clearly what your choice is and say where and what it is.
- Give reasons for your choice being a 'wonder of the world'.
- When you have written your essay, read it through again and use your checklist of personal mistakes to make sure that there are no mistakes in your writing.

READING AND USE OF ENGLISH

Part 2: Open cloze

→ workbook page 71

1 **For questions 1–8, read the text below and think of the word which best fits each gap. Use only one word in each gap. There is an example at the beginning (0).**

Reasons to be cheerful

Despite [0] ___*what*___ you may hear on the news, the future is looking bright for British teenagers. According to a government report, the economy is [1] ________ the point of making a dramatic recovery. And [2] ________ the report is correct, those who will benefit most are the young. In fact, it predicts that [3] ________ the time today's 13-year-olds leave school, unemployment will [4] ________ fallen to an all-time low. The report, which was carried [5] ________ by a leading employment agency, predicts that this growth will principally be in IT technology, because of constant technological innovation. It strongly recommends [6] ________ increase in the funding of science and technology and points out that failure to do this will mean that the UK will fall behind its competitors. The message is clear: as [7] ________ as the country continues to take education seriously, tomorrow's school leavers [8] ________ enjoy a prosperous future.

Part 3: Word formation

→ workbook page 107

2 **For questions 1–8, read the text below. Use the word given in capitals at the end of some of the lines to form a word that fits in the gap in the same line. There is an example at the beginning (0).**

The benefits of being an optimist

It is [0] ___*commonly*___ believed that it's better to be optimistic than	COMMON
pessimistic. But is that always true? Some people think that there are	
times when being pessimistic can be [1] ________ .	BENEFIT
Philosopher Alain de Botton starts with a [2] ________	CENTRE
question: what is it that causes us to be unhappy?	
And he thinks that often our [3] ________ comes from too	SAD
much hope. His [4] ________ is that in the modern age,	BELIEVE
we have learned to hope for so much that we cannot deal with the	
[5] ________ that comes when the things we hope for don't	SATISFY
happen. In this way we get put more and more pressure on ourselves.	
On the other hand, if we start from a pessimistic viewpoint, and	
have negative [6] ________ for the future, we can be	EXPECT
[7] ________ surprised when events turn out better than we'd	PLEASANT
hoped. In [8] ________, we don't feel so bad if things don't	ADD
turn out so well.	

VOCABULARY

1 Complete the sentences with the words in the list. There are four extra words.

about | apprehensive | as long as | down | dread | forward | point
succession | suppose | through | unless | up | worked | worried

1 Rishi had lots of problems, but he didn't let them get him ________________ . He stayed cheerful.
2 Sally is excited. She's ________________ to go paragliding for the first time.
3 When we were planning the trip, Leo came ________________ with some good ideas.
4 Mum said we couldn't go to the concert ________________ we got a taxi home, because it'd be late.
5 He seems so down all the time. I'm really ________________ about him.
6 ________________ you could go anywhere in the world right now – where would you go?
7 I'm feeling very ________________ about the exam tomorrow. Maths is my worst subject.
8 The organisers wanted to run ________________ the arrangements for the president's visit again.
9 I'm tired. I'm really looking ________________ to the holidays.
10 Kate was on the ________________ of leaving the house when Mr Hill phoned to cancel the meeting. /10

GRAMMAR

2 Complete the sentences with the words in the list. There are two extra words.

are going | don't | will | will be | will have | won't | would be | would have

1 If Juliana had accepted the job offer, she ________________ living in New York now.
2 By the end of the festival, I ________________ seen about 15 films.
3 Watch out! You ________________ to hit that cyclist!
4 Don't stay on the computer all night, or you ________________ feel exhausted the next day.
5 If I were taller, I ________________ been chosen for the basketball team.
6 While my parents are away on holiday, I ________________ looking after the dog.

3 Find and correct the mistake in each sentence.

1 It's Diana's birthday next Friday and she will have a party on Saturday.
2 I would have been happy if he would have come.
3 If I hadn't made so many mistakes, I would win the tennis match.
4 This time tomorrow, I'm lying on a beach in the sun.
5 If I had been taller, I wouldn't need the ladder.
6 We must finish cleaning the kitchen before our parents are arriving. /12

FUNCTIONAL LANGUAGE

4 Choose the correct options.

1 **A** Oh dear, I have *no / every* chance of saving enough money to fly to Mexico.
B Come on, look on the *better / bright* side. If you don't go to Mexico, you can buy that new phone you want.
2 **A** Yes, you can use my computer *unless / provided* you finish before six o'clock.
B That's fine! There's *any / a good* chance I'll only need it for half an hour.
3 **A** Dad won't let me watch the match *unless / as long as* I tidy my room first.
B Oh, *cheer / hang* up. Tidying your room won't take long – I'll help you!
4 **A** Yes, you can borrow my video camera *if / as long* I can use your computer for a couple of hours.
B OK, *as long / provided* as you don't spill anything on it. /8

MY SCORE /30

22–30 | 10–21 | 0–9

9 TAKE CHARGE

Get THINKING

Watch the video and think:
do you find it hard to make decisions?

OBJECTIVES

FUNCTIONS:
asking someone politely to change their behaviour

GRAMMAR:
I wish and *If only; I would prefer to / it if …, It's time, I'd rather / sooner*

VOCABULARY:
life's ups and downs; work and education

READING

1 **Look at the photos. Match each of the thoughts below to the people in the photos.**

1 *'This is so boring.'*

2 *'University life is so exciting, but I could be making money right now.'*

3 *'I'd rather spend time with my friends than go to the gym.'*

4 *'I've got the rest of my life to work.'*

2 SPEAKING **Work in pairs. Compare your answers from Exercise 1. Think of one piece of advice you could give each person.**

3 **Read the article quickly. Choose the best alternative title for the article. Discuss your ideas with a partner.**

- Decisions, Decisions, Decisions
- Keep Life Simple
- There's Always a Plan B

4 9.01 **Read and listen to the article again. Match thoughts A–G with paragraphs 1–7. Paragraphs can match with more than one thought.**

A It's better to make a decision in the morning and not at night. ☐
B I wish we didn't have to make these decisions now, while we are still so young. ☐
C You think everyone is enjoying themselves except for you. ☐
D I wish I hadn't put my social life first. ☐
E Pretend it is your friend's problem and not yours. ☐
F It is a hard decision because I'd like both things. ☐
G Things are not going well for you. ☐

5 SPEAKING **Work in pairs and discuss the questions.**

1 Which of the four pieces of advice do you think is the best? Why? Which, if any, do you disagree with?
2 Which piece of advice would be the easiest to follow, and which do you think would be the hardest?

Making difficult decisions

1 **We face decisions, big and small, throughout life. It seems unfair that there are so many major ones early on in life: exams, relationships, work, where to live … And young people are often facing these kinds of decisions for the first time, which makes it all the harder.**

2 **There are two good questions to ask yourself to help you focus: 'What is the worst that can happen?' and 'What is my Plan B if Plan A doesn't work out?' So, let's look at some difficult decisions that you might have to make.**

SCENARIO A

3 You don't want to go on that amazing new course or to a sports club on the other side of town because you'll get home late and that will get in the way of your social life. But later, will you think, 'If only I had gone on that course?' Imagine you're advising a friend. It will help you to make a rational decision rather than an emotional decision. Learning something new or exercising will do you good and you may make new friends there, too.

SCENARIO B

4 You have a more complex and less emotional decision to make. Imagine you're saving to buy a car when you are 18. Then, you see the most amazing new video game. You really want to buy it and you have enough money saved for it. However, if you buy the expensive video game, you will use your savings for the car. You wish you could afford both but you can't. You have to make a choice. Your heart says one thing and your head says another, which is tricky. How about making a list of pros and cons for both? Writing things down can be a great help. You could even colour code your notes to make sure that you're considering everything.

SCENARIO C

5 Now imagine feeling like you've let everyone down, including yourself, because you failed your exams. If only you had studied harder! But what now? Should you look for a job or repeat your exams? More studying feels like a waste of time and you're afraid you'll fail again. But now, you might end up with a low-paid, boring job and be stuck in it forever. Think through some of the possible scenarios and then try to change the way you're thinking. For instance, you might end up in a job you weren't expecting to do, but there might be advantages, too. They might even offer training or days off so you can study. If you did go back to studying and really tried your hardest, you're more likely to succeed, having learned from your mistakes.

SCENARIO D

6 You've been feeling low this year and things just don't seem to be working out the way you'd like them to. The worst thing is, you don't know how to move past it, because you can't stop thinking about it and you blame yourself for it. You keep saying, I wish I was like everyone else – they all seem to be having a great time. Try stepping back and looking at things in a simpler way. Focus on yourself and not on others. Take small decisions, one at a time. Eat breakfast, go for a walk, go to class, separate each action, don't overthink, just do.

7 In all scenarios, it's sensible to sleep on decisions. Think, and think again and then act. And remember, if you've made the wrong decision, there's always Plan B!

Train to TH!NK

Jumping to a hasty conclusion

People sometimes jump to conclusions without any evidence. Take Stefania, for example. She argued with a friend on the way to school. At school, a teacher was not happy with her homework. When she got home, she had a quarrel with her mum. Five minutes later, she was sitting in her room, thinking, 'nobody likes me'. But of course, this isn't true. To spot hasty conclusions, watch out for clue words such as all, none, most, many, always, everyone, never, sometimes, usually, hardly ever, *etc.*

6 **Read through these hasty conclusions. Why are they hasty? How can you make them true?**

1 All Brazilians love football.
2 Every teenager gets up late.
3 It always rains at the weekend.
4 People who live in big cities are less caring than people who live in the countryside.
5 Everyone loves a box of chocolates for a present.
6 Maths is hard for people who are good at languages.

7 SPEAKING **Work in groups and tell each other about some of the hasty conclusions you have heard about teenagers.**

GRAMMAR
I wish and *If only*

1 Complete the sentences with the correct forms of the verbs in the list. Check in the article on page 85. Then complete the rule.

be | can | go | study

1 I wish I ______________________ like everyone else.
2 If only I ______________________ on that course.
3 If only I ______________________ harder.
4 You wish you ______________________ afford both.

RULE: To talk about how we would like things to be different now or in the future we often use *I wish* or *if only* and the [5]______________________ tense (Sentences 1 and 4).
To talk about regrets we have about things we did in the past we often use *I wish* or *if only* and the [6]______________________ tense (Sentences 2 and 3).

2 Complete the sentences using the correct form of the verbs in brackets.

1 If only my parents ______________________ me off all the time. They just don't understand me. (not tell)
2 If only the teacher ______________________ my dad. He wouldn't be so angry with me now. (not tell)
3 I wish I ______________________ up all night. I'm so tired now. (not stay)
4 If only my football team ______________________ occasionally. Why do we always lose? (win)
5 I wish our teacher ______________________ us so much homework today. I wanted to go out this evening and now I can't. (not give)
6 If only I ______________________ to Mum and Dad. They wouldn't be so upset with me now. (not lie)
7 I wish my brother ______________________ with his mouth open. It's disgusting! (not eat)
8 I wish Annie ______________________ me to her party. Lots of my friends were invited. (invite)

3 SPEAKING **Look again at the people on page 84. Write one wish for each person. Read the wish to a partner. Can he/she guess the photos?**

→ workbook page 82

PRONUNCIATION
Linking: intrusive /w/ and /j/ Go to page 121.

VOCABULARY
Life's ups and downs

4 Match the expressions with their definitions.

1 to (not) go your way ☐
2 to blame someone or something ☐
3 to let someone down ☐
4 to try your hardest ☐
5 to get in the way of something ☐
6 to dwell on something ☐
7 to (not) work out the way we'd like them to ☐
8 to be tricky ☐

a to disappoint someone
b to do your best
c to think about something for a long time (often meaning you can't make a decision about it)
d when the results of something are(n't) what we'd hoped for
e to be difficult
f to say something is someone's fault
g to obstruct or prevent something
h when things happen (or don't happen) the way you want them to

5 Complete the text with the correct form of expressions of Exercise 4.

OK, so I made a mistake. I shouldn't have been playing football in the house. Now the window's broken – that's certainly going to [1]______________________ my plans for a house party this weekend. It is a very [2]______________________ situation. Mum and Dad are going to say I've [3]______________________ them ______________________ and that I'm not responsible enough to be left alone in the house. Well, I didn't [4]______________________ it for too long and decided to try and do something to make them proud. I decided to make dinner. I [5]______________________ my ______________________, I really did, but things have [6]______________________ and the pie's a bit of a disappointment. I mean I thought it was going to be a beautiful golden brown colour like in the book, but mine is black all over. I [7]______________________ the oven. I think it's hotter than it says it is. And then the chip pan. I mean how did that catch fire? Some days nothing seems to [8]______________________. Oh well, the table looks nice. Although that candle does look a bit close to the curtains. Oh, dear! I need some water. Quick!

→ workbook page 84

LISTENING

6 SPEAKING **Work in pairs. Look at the photos of three 19-year-olds and discuss the questions.**

1 What do they do?
2 How are their lives similar and how are they different?
3 How do you imagine they feel about their future?

7 9.04 **Listen to a radio programme. Which of the three life choices in the photos in Exercise 6 does Jo, a careers advisor, recommend that Alex pursues next year?**

8 9.04 **Listen again and choose the correct answer A, B or C.**

1 What kind of job do approximately a third of students get?
  A one that requires more training
  B one that is boring
  C one that doesn't require a degree
2 Why is university no longer a very tempting option?
  A It takes longer to get a degree.
  B It is very expensive.
  C It is difficult to get a job after university.
3 What does Jo tell Alex?
  A He should definitely go to university.
  B He should follow his parents' advice.
  C There is an alternative way to get a degree.
4 What are half of today's young people keen to do?
  A work in business management
  B set up their own company
  C do a degree in business studies at university
5 What is Jo's advice to Gemma about setting up a business?
  A to organise events for her customers
  B to understand her customers and their likes and dislikes
  C to follow her customers on Instagram and Twitter

VOCABULARY

Work and education

9 Match the words with the definitions.

1 work experience ☐
2 a school leaver ☐
3 careers advisor ☐
4 apprenticeship ☐
5 a degree ☐
6 a graduate ☐
7 life experience ☐
8 launch your own business ☐

a practical wisdom gained from living
b experience of having a job
c set up or start a company
d someone who has recently finished school
e training whilst you work
f someone who has recently finished university
g a qualification you get from a college or university
h someone who gives advice about work and further studies

10 Complete the paragraph using the words from Exercise 9. You can only use each word or phrase once.

I won't finish school for another two years, but I'm already a bit worried about what to do. It would be good to get some [1]__________, but there aren't a lot of good jobs for [2]__________, so I think I'll go to university and try to get a [3]__________. It'll be much easier to find work as a [4]__________. I'm not sure what I want to study yet, and I've heard that an [5]__________ might be a good option, as it involves on-the-job-training, so I'm going to see a [6]__________ to get some advice about all of this. Anyway, I'm not sure I want to go straight into a career. It would be nice to have a year out and get some [7]__________. Or maybe I'll see if I can [8]__________. I've got lots of ideas and I think it's a great way to make lots of money – if you do it right.

→ workbook page 84

SPEAKING

11 Read the sentences and write A (agree) or D (disagree). Discuss the statements in small groups.

1 It's a good idea to get work experience when you're still at school. ☐
2 All students should see a careers advisor before they leave school. ☐
3 University isn't for everyone. ☐
4 It's important to get a good degree to be successful in life. ☐
5 Doing a degree course is too expensive. ☐

What kind of a FRIEND are you?

We all need friends, or do we? Maybe it depends on whether they're a good friend or a bad friend. What kind of friend are you? Take our quiz and find out …

1 What would you do if someone was gossiping about your best friend?

a I'd say nothing.
b I'd speak out and say, 'I'd prefer it if you didn't talk about Jane like that.'
c I'd join in and agree with them.

2 How often do your friends come to you for advice?

a occasionally, for practical advice
b all the time
c never

3 If you saw a boy from your class sitting alone in the canteen what would you do?

a I'd think, 'Poor guy, but he's so boring.'
b I'd choose to go and sit with him.
c I'd sooner ignore him and go and sit with my friends.

4 The most important thing about friendship is …

a Who needs friends when there's Netflix to watch?
b always being there for each other and being able to share your feelings.
c having people who like all your posts on social media!

5 Your friend Lucy says she's got the Saturday job you had also applied for. How do you react?

a You say you don't understand why she got it.
b You're very happy for her and say, 'It's about time something nice happened to you.' Then you congratulate her.
c Nothing. You feel jealous and walk off angrily.

6 You are on holiday with a group of friends. One friend wants to go swimming, another wants to go for a walk and the third wants to play tennis. What would you say or do?

a I'd rather say nothing and put my headphones on and wait for my friends to decide.
b I'd try to make sure that everyone got to do what they wanted to do.
c I'd say, 'I'd prefer to go swimming, so let's go swimming.'

READING

1 9.05 Read and listen to the quiz from a teen magazine and choose your answers.

2 SPEAKING Compare your answers in pairs.

3 Read the key. Do you agree with the advice? Do you think this is a fair description of you? Why (not)?

4 WRITING Work in pairs. Write three more questions for the quiz.

Mostly a's

You're not such a good friend, because you're a bit of a loner. You don't like drama and you are not a very supportive friend.

Mostly b's

You're very kind and considerate. In fact, you're the kind of friend everyone needs.

Mostly c's

Oh, dear. You really aren't a very good friend at all. You are really quite selfish. You always put yourself before your friends.

GRAMMAR

Grammar video ▶ 24

I would prefer to / it if, It's time, I'd rather / sooner

5 Choose the correct option. Check your answers in the quiz on page 88. Then read the rule and match each point to the five sentences.

a I'd rather *say / said* nothing.
b I'd sooner *ignore / ignored* him and sit with my friends.
c It's about time something nice *happen / happened* to you.
d I'd prefer it if you *don't / didn't* talk about Jane like that.
e I'd prefer *to go / going* swimming.

> **RULE:** To say we think someone should do something, we can use:
> *It's time* + subject + past simple — sentence [1] ___
> To talk about our own preference, we can use:
> *I'd rather / sooner* + base form — sentence [2] ___
> *I'd prefer* + infinitive — sentence [3] ___
> If the subject of the second verb is different from the subject of *'d rather / sooner / prefer*, we use:
> *I'd rather / sooner* + subject + past tense
> *I'd prefer it if* + subject + past tense — sentence [4] ___

6 Complete the sentences with the correct form of one of the verbs in the list.

eat | go | learn | leave | not invite | not tell | play | stay in

1 I'm not really keen on listening to opera in the car. I'd rather you ______________ something else.
2 It's a secret. I'd prefer it if you ______________ anyone else.
3 I'm tired. It's about time I ______________ to bed.
4 I don't really like Tim. I'd sooner you ______________ him to the party.
5 We had Italian food last week. I'd rather ______________ at the Chinese restaurant tonight.
6 I don't want to miss the train. I'd sooner ______________ the house a bit earlier.
7 Can't you make yourself something to eat? It really is time you ______________ to cook.
8 I don't really want to go out. I'd prefer ______________ tonight.

→ workbook page 83

FUNCTIONS

Asking someone politely to change their behaviour

7 Look at the picture and complete the conversation with a suitable verb.

Mum	Josh. I'd rather you [1]______________ your phone at the table.
Josh	Sorry, Mum. I won't be a minute.
Mum	And I'd sooner you [2]______________ with your mouth open.
Josh	I'll try not to.
Mum	And I'd prefer it if you [3]______________ your feet on the floor, not on the table.
Josh	OK, Mum. Is there anything I can do?
Mum	Yes, you can improve your table manners!

8 WRITING Use the picture below and the expressions in Exercise 7 to write a short conversation between the passenger and the driver.

SPEAKING

It's not always good to be entirely truthful, especially when you could hurt someone's feelings or cause an argument. In these cases, it's better to try and find a way of being 'diplomatic' and to say something that won't cause offence.

9 Work in pairs. Decide on the best way to handle each of these situations. What would you say in each one?

1 Your mum and dad have made plans for a family visit to your grandparents this Saturday. They've forgotten that you've got a school football match that day.
2 You're at a friend's house having dinner. His father serves you fish. You really don't like fish.
3 Your friend wants to join the school volleyball team, but you know that she/he isn't good enough to play for the team.
4 Your teacher asks the class to come up with ideas for a school trip. A friend comes up with an idea, but you don't think it's a good idea and you think you have a better one.

Literature

1 **Look at the photos and read the introduction to the extract. Do you think you would like to read the book?**

The Remains of the Day by Kazuo Ishiguro

Stevens has spent his life as a butler, working for Lord Darlington. He is now an elderly man. At the end of the book, he finds himself sitting alone on a bench, on a pier at the seaside. A stranger begins to talk to him, and Stevens starts to tell the man about his life and his feelings about Lord Darlington.

'You must have been very attached to this Lord whatever. And it's three years since he passed away, you say? I can see you were very attached to him, mate.'

'Lord Darlington wasn't a bad man. He wasn't a bad man at all. And at least he had the privilege of being able to say at the end of his life that he made his own mistakes. His lordship was a courageous man. He chose a certain path in life, it proved to be a misguided one, but there, he chose it, he can say that at least. As for myself, I can't even claim that. You see, I trusted. I trusted in his lordship's wisdom. All those years I served him, I trusted I was doing something worthwhile. I can't even say I made my own mistakes. Really – one has to ask oneself – what dignity is there in that?'

'Now, look, mate, I'm not sure I follow everything you're saying. But if you ask me, your attitude's all wrong, see? Don't keep looking back all the time, you're bound to get depressed. And all right, you can't do your job as well as you used to. But it's the same for all of us, see? We've all got to put our feet up at some point. Look at me. Been happy as a lark since the day I retired. All right, so neither of us are exactly in our first flush of youth, but you've got to keep looking forward.'

And I believe it was then that he said:

'You've got to enjoy yourself. The evening's the best part of the day. You've done your day's work. Now you can put your feet up and enjoy it. That's how I look at it. Ask anybody, they'll all tell you. The evening's the best part of the day.' […]

It is now some twenty minutes since the man left, but I have remained here on this bench to await the event that has just taken place – namely, the switching on of the pier lights. As I say, the happiness with which the pleasure-seekers gathering on this pier greeted this small event would tend to vouch for the correctness of my companion's words; for a great many people, the evening is the most enjoyable part of the day. Perhaps, then, there is something to his advice that I should cease looking back so much, that I should adopt a more positive outlook and try to make the best of whatever remains of my day. After all, what can we ever gain in forever looking back and blaming ourselves if our lives have not turned out quite as we might have wished? […] What is the point in worrying oneself too much about what one could or could not have done to control the course one's life took? Surely it is enough that the likes of you and me at least try to make our small contribution count for something true and worthy. And if some of us are prepared to sacrifice much in life in order to pursue such aspirations, surely that is in itself, whatever the outcome, cause for pride and contentment.

2 **Read the extract quickly and decide what seems to confirm the theory that the evening is the best part of the day.**

a the switching on of the pier lights
b the fact that the people on the pier are enjoying themselves
c knowing that your day's work is done

3 9.06 **Read and listen to the extract again. Who do these sentences refer to? Write LD (Lord Darlington), S (Stevens) or M (the man).**

1 He made his own mistakes in life. ☐
2 He didn't choose his own path in life. ☐
3 He is happy in his retirement. ☐
4 He died three years ago. ☐
5 He is no longer a young man. ☐

4 VOCABULARY **Match the highlighted words in the extract with the definitions.**

1 the quality of a person that makes him or her deserving of respect
2 the part someone plays to make something successful
3 things you hope to accomplish
4 died
5 the male head of a household staff
6 try to achieve something
7 wrong because of bad judgment or false information
8 meaningful

5 SPEAKING **Work in pairs and discuss the questions.**

1 Does Stevens have a positive or negative outlook? Give examples.
2 What can he do to change his outlook? Do you have any advice for him?
3 Is there anything you look back on and regret? Why?

WRITING
A magazine article

1 INPUT **Read Eve's article and answer the questions.**

1 Does she agree with the statement?
2 What are her main arguments to support her position?

Students should try to get some work experience before they go to university

Do you really want to spend the rest of your life either studying or working? Wouldn't you like the chance to do a little more with your life and find out what it is you really want?

Most young people who have decided to go to university or college go straight from school. A few people may take a gap year to see a bit of the world or earn some money, but how many take five or six years, or even longer before they go on to study more?

These days, young people are led to believe that the pressures in the labour market are so high that they cannot afford to waste any time doing things that won't directly help them get a good job. They feel that if they haven't graduated by the age of 22, they will be too old to be successful.

This is simply not true. Graduates are feeling the pressure precisely because so many of them are looking for the same jobs at the same time and there's very little for an employer to choose between them.

Anyone who is brave enough to wait some years before they go to university will – as long as they have used their time well – be far more attractive as an employee. Their extra experience of life will mean they can offer companies so much more than any fresh-faced 22-year-old can. Besides, the fact that they've taken time to decide exactly what it is they wanted to do, shows that now they really want to do it.

So go on. Be brave. Delay. Go out and find out a little more about life. After all, you've got the rest of your life to work.

2 ANALYSE **Look at the first and last paragraphs of the article. What technique does Eve use in each one? What effect does this have on the reader?**

3 PLAN **Choose one of the topics below. What is your position? What are your main arguments to support your position? Write notes.**

- Doing a degree course is a waste of money.
- The government should pay for all students to study at university or college.

My position	
Argument 1	
Argument 2	
Argument 3	

4 **You're going to write an article for your school magazine about the topic you chose in Exercise 3. Think carefully about how to start and finish it.**

1 Think of two direct questions you could use to start the article.
2 Think of two imperatives to conclude your article.

5 PRODUCE **Write your article (200–250 words).**

10 UNBELIEVABLE NEWS

OBJECTIVES

FUNCTIONS: making a point; introducing news

GRAMMAR: reported speech (review); reported questions and requests

VOCABULARY: sharing news; reporting verbs

Get THINKING

Watch the video and think: is gossiping always bad?

A

B

C

D

E

READING

1 **Look at the photos. How are these people getting or giving news? Can you think of any other ways of giving or getting news?**

2 SPEAKING **Work in pairs. Match these opinions with the photos in Exercise 1. They can go with more than one photo. Is each one an advantage or a disadvantage?**

1 It takes ages.
2 You can read what you want, when you want.
3 You can share information easily.
4 You can trust the information you get.
5 You have to be careful what you read and write.
6 You can't always get reception.

3 SPEAKING **With your partner, think of more advantages and disadvantages related to each of the different ways of sharing news in Exercise 1. Compare with another pair.**

4 10.01 **Read and listen to the magazine article. What are the four main research results about 'fake news'?**

5 **Read the text again. Six phrases have been removed. Choose from A–G the phrase which fits each gap (1–6). There is one extra phrase.**

A the research results are a little disturbing
B unless the research confirms it
C that they are not taken in by it
D assessing whether something is true or not
E because you saw it one place
F showing that it spreads way faster than the truth
G they touch people's hopes and fears

6 SPEAKING **Work in pairs and discuss the questions.**

1 What most interested/surprised/concerned you in the article?
2 Do you always believe what people say on social media? Do you check important information that comes to you through social media? How?
3 Should people be worried about 'fake news'? Why (not)?

FAKE NEWS

The rise in the last decade or so of 'fake news' has also led to increased research into what it is, how it spreads and what its effects are.

Many people believe that they can spot 'fake news' and [1] ________________ . One of the most worrying research discoveries is that this is not really true. Many studies have shown that we become more willing to believe something if we read or hear it enough times – and that includes things that we start off not believing. Back in 2015, some researchers in the US gave students statements which they were told were very likely to be false. When the statements were repeated several times, however, many students became uncertain. The lead researcher said that repeating something often enough made some students begin to think it was true. The 'good news' from the research is that our knowledge is still a strong factor in determining what we believe or disbelieve. However, since there's so much fake news going around these days, [2] ________________ .

What adds to the feeling that we should be worried about fake news is further research [3] ________________ . A ten-year study with three million Twitter users followed the spread of over 120,000 Twitter stories (a 'story' was a tweet that made a statement about something outside the user's own life – the statements were fact-checked by independent organisations). A researcher said that they had found some frightening things – especially the fact that truthful tweets took six times longer to spread to other Twitter users than fake ones.

It's clear that people who produce fake news know that people love headlines and statements that shock, that disgust, that are scary. This is one reason why people are more likely to share them – [4] ________________ . One researcher said that often people share something, not because they necessarily thought it was true, but because it would make friends and people in their network react strongly.

But surely, now, after basically two decades of the internet and social media, people are much better at [5] ________________ ? Apparently not. Recently, American high-school students were given a photo of a damaged flower. The researchers told them it was a flower from near a damaged nuclear power plant, but did not tell them what the source of the photo was. Forty percent of the students thought the photo was good evidence about the state of the area around the nuclear plant, even though they had no idea where it came from.

So if you want to get real, not fake, news, check where it comes from. If it's a shared piece, who's sharing it with you and why? If it's from a website, have a look at the stories on the site – if they're all shocking or scandalous stories, be careful. And generally, never accept something's true [6] ________________ : see if you can find it in other – trustworthy – places, too.

Train to TH!NK

Recognising the source of a statement

It's good to get an idea of the background of the person who says or writes something. Are they an impartial expert or are they someone who wants to change your opinion to suit their own agenda? For example, this statement about a flu epidemic, 'Patients can already spread the virus a day before they've fallen sick themselves,' is more likely to have come from a doctor than from a politician. On the other hand, 'We have to stop people who are carrying the virus from getting into the country' is more likely to come from a politician. By knowing who is providing a piece of information, you're better able to decide how much importance to give it and whether you can really trust what they say.

7 SPEAKING **Read these statements about social media. Match them with the person you think said them. Which do you think is the least trustworthy? Why? Discuss in pairs.**

1 a psychologist | **2** a politician | **3** a linguist | **4** an IT expert | **5** an advertising executive

a We have noticed that people use fewer abbreviations on Twitter than in texting, and tweets seem to show more creative word use.

b Young people sometimes make things public that they regret later. This can cause emotional problems as well as a feeling of helplessness.

c We're trying to develop a system that will help people to upload multiple photos faster.

d We use social media in order to spread our key messages more efficiently.

e Twitter – quite simply the most effective way to reach our target consumers.

GRAMMAR
Reported speech (review)

1 Read these examples of reported speech and rewrite them in direct speech. Then complete the rule.

1 The researchers told them it was a flower from near a damaged nuclear power plant.
2 A researcher said that they had found some frightening things.
3 One researcher said that often people didn't share something because they necessarily thought it was true.

RULE: When we report what someone has said we often change the verb tense.

present simple ➜ *past simple*
present continuous ➜ [4] ______
present perfect ➜ [5] ______
past simple ➜ [6] ______
will ➜ [7] ______
can ➜ [8] ______

We also change certain other words.

here ➜ there
now ➜ [9] ______
this ➜ [10] ______
today ➜ [11] ______
tomorrow ➜ [12] ______
yesterday ➜ [13] ______
tonight ➜ [14] ______

Don't forget to change any pronouns so that they agree with any subject changes, e.g *my* ➜ *his/her*.

2 Report these messages that you've received.

1 I'll be in town later this evening.
He ______.
2 We had a great time at your house yesterday. Thanks.
They ______.
3 I'm missing you. I can't wait for tomorrow!
She ______.
4 John's missed his train. He's going to be late.
John's mum ______.
5 I'm seeing Eva tonight. I'll tell her when I see her.
Becca ______.
6 The baby's due today!
Lucas ______.

3 WRITING **Write four messages about your day and plans for the future for a partner to report.**

➜ workbook page 90

VOCABULARY
Sharing news

4 Match the phrases with their meanings.

1 I'll let you know as soon as I hear anything. ☐
2 If you see Ling, can you pass on the message? ☐
3 An old friend of mine got in touch with me on Instagram the other day. ☐
4 It's so easy to keep in touch with all your friends these days. ☐
5 When you tell her, break the news gently. ☐
6 His followers retweeted his message more than 10,000 times. ☐
7 I'll drop you a line when we get there. ☐
8 Give me a call when you get home. ☐

a tell him
b stay in contact
c sent on / forwarded (via Twitter)
d send you a message
e phone me
f tell you
g made contact
h tell her what's happened

5 Complete the questions with suitable verbs.

1 If you're going to be home late, how do you ______ your parents know?
2 How do you prefer to ______ good or bad news to other people?
3 How do you ______ in touch with your friends from primary school?
4 How do you ______ in touch with old friends who you're not currently in contact with?
5 What's the best way to ______ bad news?
6 Have you ever ______ someone else's message on Twitter?
7 When was the last time you ______ someone a line and what did you say?
8 Do you always ______ your best friend a call on their birthday? I usually send them a text.

6 SPEAKING **Work in pairs and discuss the questions from Exercise 5.**

➜ workbook page 92

PRONUNCIATION
Linking: omission of the /h/ sound
Go to page 121.

LISTENING

7 SPEAKING **You are going to listen to an interview with Janice Gordon, a foreign correspondent. What do you think her job involves? Compare your ideas in pairs.**

8 10.04 **Janice is being interviewed about her work by a group of students at a careers fair. Listen to the interview and mark the sentences T (true) or F (false).**

1 A lot of the time, Janice is not at home. ☐
2 Her work is always dangerous. ☐
3 Sometimes, she would prefer to be a reporter in an office. ☐
4 In some cases it's important that she's physically fit. ☐
5 Not everyone trusts her reports are an accurate reflection of what happened. ☐
6 She thinks she is lucky to have her job. ☐

9 10.04 **Listen again and answer the questions.**

1 What does a correspondent have to do to 'get a really good story'?
2 How does Janice rely on the help of local people in her work?
3 What does she sometimes have to do in order to get fit?
4 She mentions one thing she didn't enjoy. What was it?
5 Does she recommend her job? Why (not)?

10 SPEAKING **Work in pairs and discuss the questions.**

1 Would you like to be a foreign correspondent? Why (not)?
2 Which place(s) do you think would be the most difficult for Janice to go to right now? Why?

GRAMMAR

Grammar video ▶26

Reported questions and requests

11 Here are three sentences from the interview with Janice. Which are questions and which are requests? Write the direct questions and complete the rule with *requests*, *yes/no questions* or *wh- questions*.

1 You asked me if my job was dangerous.
2 He asked me to run ten kilometres.
3 Just now, someone asked me why I do [this job].

a 'Is ________________________ ?'
b 'Can ________________________ , please?'
c 'Why ________________________ ?'

RULE: In reported [4]________________________ , we use *if* or *whether* and the same word order as in a statement.
In reported [5]________________________ , we use the question word and the same word order as in a statement. We do not use auxiliaries.
In reported [6]________________________ , we use *asked* + person + infinitive.

12 Here are more questions the students asked Janice. Write them as reported speech. Be careful with the word order.

0 'When did you start this job?'
One of the students asked her when she had started that job.
1 'Which newspaper do you work for?'
2 'Where are you going next?'
3 'Have you ever been scared in your job?'
4 'Is your job well-paid?'
5 'Who is your boss?'

→ workbook page 91

SPEAKING

13 Work in groups of four. Imagine you are journalists. You are going to interview some well-known people you have never met before. Agree together on four people. For each person, write four or five questions to ask them.

14 Act out the interviews. One of you is the famous person. The others ask questions and write down the answers.

15 Each group reports to the class about the group's interviews.

We talked to Harry Styles.

We asked him when he started singing. He said he had always sung ...

WRITING

A magazine article

16 Write a magazine article about one of your interviews. Make sure you do these things. Write 200-250 words.

- Give a short introduction to the person.
- Say why you chose to interview this person.
- Include reported questions and statements.

The Secret Paparazzo

We continue our **'secret professional'** series with an offering from an anonymous paparazzo.

A I've always loved cameras and photographs. After I left school, I worked with a local photographer, then a bit later for a newspaper. One day, the editor said he wanted some photos of a famous person who lived nearby and I agreed to go and get them. I got some good photos, and a big national newspaper bought them, too. I thought, 'OK, this is how I can make good money.'

B That's how my life as a paparazzo started. (By the way, that's the singular – paparazzi is plural.) Paparazzi are not the most popular people in the world – especially after what happened to Princess Diana – but I've never regretted taking up the profession. And I've never denied being a paparazzo. That said, when I meet people I just say I'm a photographer and leave it at that. It's easier that way.

C I never apologise for doing what I do, because I don't think I need to. I take photos of famous people (often without them knowing, it's true) and then sell the photos to magazines. If people didn't buy those magazines, I wouldn't be able to sell the photos. I provide a service and I'm not ashamed of it. I love my job. I like the money, but I also like the challenge, the fact that you have to know where the celebrity's going to be. You have to be technically good, too – not everyone can take a good photo of someone at a distance.

D People have accused me of doing an unpleasant thing – but I honestly don't think it is. I take photos and sell them. Am I telling lies? Stealing? Attacking people? No, and in fact I've always argued that celebrities don't mind as much as you might think. A famous person once admitted to me that they often leaked information about where they were so the paparazzi could get photos. The old saying is: all publicity is good publicity, and they know it. You can tell me that celebrities don't want their private lives invaded, but you can't tell me they don't love publicity.

E I can understand, though, why paparazzi get some bad press sometimes. Not all of my colleagues are as ethical as they might be. We've often been criticised for taking photos of young children – something I don't do, by the way – and quite right, too. And should we take photos of people when they're ill? When they're at a funeral? I've got my views, some of my colleagues have got theirs. But then we're just like bankers or lawyers, aren't we?

F The profession is different now. A colleague warned me years ago that social media would change things, and she was right. I use it a lot. I follow celebrities' posts and they help me find out where they are. It helps with legal issues, too. It used to be much harder for us! For example, celebrity X finds a photo of themselves somewhere and posts it on social media – only, the photo was taken by a paparazzo who says, 'That photo's mine and you need permission to use it! So, be prepared to pay for it, or you can't use it!'

READING

1 SPEAKING **You are going to read an article by a member of the paparazzi. What do you know about paparazzi? Tell a partner.**

2 10.05 **Read and listen to the article. Match paragraphs A–F with titles 1–7. There is one extra title you do not need to use.**

1 Morally OK? ☐
2 Why I love it ☐
3 Things have changed ☐
4 Starting out ☐
5 The future of paparazzi ☐
6 It isn't dishonest ☐
7 No regrets ☐

3 **Read the article again and mark the sentences T (true), F (false) or DS (doesn't say). Then correct the false sentences.**

1 He learned about cameras and photography at school. ☐
2 He avoids telling people he's a paparazzo. ☐
3 He thinks anyone could do what he does. ☐
4 He believes that celebrities hate being photographed. ☐
5 He doesn't take photos of sick children. ☐
6 He has sued celebrities who used his photographs. ☐

4 SPEAKING **Work in pairs and discuss the questions.**

1 What questions would you ask the paparazzo if you met him?
2 Do you know of any controversial events concerning paparazzi?

VOCABULARY
Reporting verbs

5 Complete the examples with verbs from the list, using the article to help you. Then complete the rule with the verbs.

accused | admitted | agreed | apologise | argued
criticised | denied | regretted | warned

1 He ______________ to go and take some photos for the newspaper.
2 He has never ______________ deciding to become a paparazzo.
3 He's never ______________ being a paparazzo.
4 He doesn't ______________ for doing what he does.
5 People have ______________ him of being part of an unpleasant profession.
6 He's always ______________ that celebrities aren't too worried about being photographed.
7 A celebrity ______________ that they wanted the paparazzi to know where they were.
8 Paparazzi have been ______________ for taking photographs of children.
9 A friend of his ______________ him that things were going to change.

RULE: Different reporting verbs are followed by different verb patterns. Here are some of the more common ones.

pattern	examples
+ (*that*) + clause	argue / [10] ______________
+ [person] + (*that*) + clause	[11] ______________
+ infinitive	[12] ______________
+ gerund	regret / [13] ______________
+ *for* + gerund	apologise / [14] ______________
+ [person] + *of* + gerund	[15] ______________

6 Report these sentences using the verbs in brackets.

1 It was me. I took your sandwich. (admit)
2 I didn't do it. I didn't steal the money. (deny)
3 You did it. You told Jim my secret! (accuse)
4 Don't touch that dog. It bites! (warn)
5 I wish I hadn't said those things. I really do. (regret)
6 I'm really sorry I broke your phone. (apologise)
7 You drive so badly. Can't you slow down? (criticise)
8 Sure, I'll take you to the party. (agree)
9 I think it's important to always tell the truth. (argue)

→ workbook page 92

FUNCTIONS
Making a point

7 10.06 Read the news story below. Listen to two different newspaper editors saying what they think about it. Which editor, 1 or 2, wants to run the story?

A woman, who was once on a reality TV show and has kept her name in the papers ever since, by saying outrageous things, has caused controversy again by tweeting something rude about the Queen.

8 10.06 Listen again. How do the editors justify their views? Who do you agree with more?

9 10.06 Put the words in order to make sentences. Then listen again and check.

1 news / way / There's / story / this / is / no / a
2 story / really / running / against / I'm / this
3 up / My / made / mind's
4 want / is / exactly / of / This / the / kind / story / we
5 definitely / We're / with / story / going / this
6 final / that's / And\

WordWise: Expressions with *way*

10 Look at these sentences from the unit so far. Complete them with phrases from the list.

all the way | have it both ways | in a way |
no way | one way or another | way too

1 I think it's ______________ easy to make that kind of criticism.
2 I'm with you ______________ on that, Pete.
3 You can't ______________, you know.
4 ______________, it's the same thing as inventing stuff, isn't it?
5 ______________, we're talking about dishonesty.
6 There's ______________ this is a news story.

11 Match the phrases in Exercise 10 with these meanings.

a partly ☐
b very/really ☐
c no possibility ☐
d completely/as much as possible ☐
e benefit from two completely opposite things ☐
f from one perspective ☐

→ workbook page 92

DEVELOPING SPEAKING

1 10.07 **Look at the photo. What's happening? Read and listen to check.**

Bea: Hi Luke. You're late. What kept you?

Luke: It's none of your business, Bea.

Bea: Wow! You're in a bad mood. Have you had some bad news or something?

Luke: No, not bad news, but you're right; I'm not in a good mood. I'm embarrassed and angry at myself. You'll never guess what happened to me. I got stopped in the street, that local TV news programme was there with a camera crew and an interviewer. She said, 'So, what do you think about the plans for the new shopping centre?' And all I could say was, 'What new shopping centre?' Everyone laughed. It was so embarrassing. My big chance to be on TV and I blew it!

Bea: Hah, hah, hah! That's so funny! 'What new shopping centre?' Brilliant! Oh come on, Luke – you've got to try to see the funny side of it.

Luke: I guess, but it's not easy when you've made a fool of yourself.

Bea: Oh, don't worry. No one knows about it – except me, of course! But how on earth do you not know about the shopping centre plans? Don't you follow the news?

Luke: I do. Well, I look at things on Twitter sometimes, at least. But I've been so busy lately, what with exams and everything. In any case, why haven't we been discussing it at school? There's a current affairs lesson every week, isn't there?

Bea: Those lessons aren't about local stuff, you know that. We talk about climate change and world politics, not new shopping centres. But I can tell you all about it if you like.

Luke: Don't bother. It's too late now. I mean, they're not going to ask me again, are they?

Bea: No, but you might want to know what's going on in your own hometown.

2 10.07 **Read and listen to the dialogue again and answer the questions.**

1. Why was Luke embarrassed by his answer?
2. What is Bea surprised about?
3. What are the current affairs lessons at their school about?

3 SPEAKING **Discuss the statements in pairs. Do you agree with them?**

1. What happened to Luke was really embarrassing.
2. Teenagers should follow local news as well as global news.

Phrases for fluency

4 **Find the underlined expressions in the dialogue and use them to complete the sentences.**

1. Why ____________ did you dye your hair green?
2. Can you lend me £20? Or £5, ____________ ?
3. There's no wi-fi in the camp where we're going, so ____________ writing me any emails.
4. I'm bored. Let's go swimming ____________ .
5. I don't really want to go to the party, and ____________ I haven't been invited.
6. Stop asking me questions! It's ____________ !

5 SPEAKING **Work in pairs. Student A is someone who thinks it's important to follow the news. Student B doesn't watch or listen to the news. Write a short conversation and then act it out.**

FUNCTIONS
Introducing news

KEY LANGUAGE

You'll never believe ...	Did you know that ...?
Have you heard (about) ...?	Guess what?

6 **Complete each sentence with one word.**

1. ____________ what? I got 90 percent in the test!
2. Did you ____________ that Maura's moving to Australia?
3. You'll never ____________ what happened to me yesterday.
4. Have you ____________ about Mike? He's broken his leg.

7 SPEAKING **Work in pairs. Think of three surprising pieces of news (real or invented). Then follow the instructions below. Use the phrases in the Key Language box.**

- A tells a piece of news to B using a phrase above.
- B replies.
- Then switch roles.

LIFE COMPETENCIES

We all do or say foolish things sometimes, and people laugh at us – a healthy reaction to such situations is to laugh at yourself, too. Laughing at yourself can help you stop feeling embarrassed.

1 ▶ 27 **Watch the vlog. What is the punchline to Will's final joke?**

2 ▶ 27 **Watch the vlog again and answer the questions.**

1 Why does Will start by telling jokes?
2 Who calls him halfway through the vlog?
3 What 'mistake' has Will made?

3 **Read the stories. Imagine you are the person in each one. Put the situations in order of how embarrassing you think they are.**

A One day I got on an empty bus with my headphones on. I closed my eyes and started singing along. Suddenly someone tapped me on the shoulder, and a lady said 'Can you sing more quietly please?' There were about five other people on the bus now, all laughing or smiling. I felt really stupid! MAGGIE

B I was in a clothes shop with my family. I found a pair of jeans and I went over to where my dad was paying for some things. I put the jeans down and said: 'Can you pay for these, too?' The man turned round, smiled and said: 'Well, I'm very sorry, but no!' Of course, it wasn't my dad. I looked away and saw my sister, laughing like crazy. CARLOS

C My dad bought a new car and drove to the supermarket. After doing the shopping, he pressed the key to open the car – nothing. He put the key in the lock – nothing. Dad got angry and kicked the tyre of the car. Just then a woman came up and asked him what he was doing. Dad looked at her and then at the number plate – it wasn't his car. ANDREA

4 SPEAKING **Work in pairs. Compare your ideas from Exercise 3.**

5 SPEAKING **Read the responses below. With your partner, choose the best response for each person, A, B or C. Say why you think it's the best one.**

Maggie
A get off the bus as quickly as possible
B smile and say, 'Sorry, I'm a terrible singer!'
C put your headphones back on and start listening again without singing

Carlos
A tell your sister to stop laughing at you
B turn around and walk away
C smile and say, 'Well, I feel really silly, I'm sorry!'

Andrea's dad
A laugh and tell the woman you've made a mistake
B run to your car and drive away quickly
C say you thought there was a problem with the tyre on her car and were trying to help

Me and my world

6 **Think of a time when you did or said something foolish or embarrassing and make notes.**

- What happened?
- Why was it embarrassing?
- How did you react? Do you think it would have been better if you had reacted differently?

7 SPEAKING **Work in pairs and tell your partner about the situation. Then discuss these questions.**

1 Why might laughing at yourself be the best response?
2 Do you know anyone who is good at laughing at their own behaviour or embarrassment?
3 How do you usually react when you have done or said something embarrassing?

TIPS FOR LAUGHING AT YOURSELF

- If you do something embarrassing and people laugh, remember that they're laughing at what happened more than laughing at you.
- Try to smile first – this helps you deal with the embarrassment.
- If you can laugh at something you've done, remember: other people will then be laughing with you, not at you.

B2 First for Schools

LISTENING

Part 4: Multiple choice → workbook page 89

1 10.08 **You will hear an interview with a teenager called Diana Hollingsworth about the 'Good News Project'. For questions 1–7, choose the best answer (A, B or C).**

1 Diana's main reason for starting the project was that she
- **A** was fed up of hearing only bad news.
- **B** was determined to stop people complaining about the news.
- **C** wanted to change the way her school magazine reported stories.

2 What did the local newspaper initially agree to do?
- **A** to see if it would be popular with their readers
- **B** to teach her about journalism
- **C** to publish five stories each week

3 What does Diana say she enjoys about preparing stories for the radio station?
- **A** finding unusual ideas
- **B** making people laugh
- **C** hearing her voice on the radio

4 What does Diana find most difficult about the project?
- **A** co-ordinating her team of reporters
- **B** deciding which stories to give to the newspaper and radio station
- **C** checking that the stories are true

5 What should someone do if they have a story for the project?
- **A** write it up and send it in
- **B** be sure that it is recent
- **C** give it to one of the pupils at Diana's school

6 How has Diana's opinion of the world changed?
- **A** She has realised there are more good people than bad people.
- **B** She now feels more optimistic about the future.
- **C** She has become confident she can make a difference.

7 What are Diana's favourite kind of good news stories about?
- **A** funny things that pets do
- **B** helping people in the local community
- **C** people overcoming serious problems

WRITING

Part 2: A review → workbook page 25

2 **You have seen this advert on a website for teenagers. Write your review in 140–190 words in an appropriate style.**

Reviews wanted

We are looking for reviews of a news website that you use regularly. Tell us why you use it and what type of information you can find on it. Is the website easy to use? Who would you recommend it to and why?
The best reviews will be published next month.

VOCABULARY

1 Complete the sentences with the words in the list. There are four extra words.

admitted | apologise | break | careers | degree | drop
front | give | let | live | living | pass | regretted | way

1 Maddy wants to work in finance so she is applying for a ________________ course at university.
2 The programme was kind of interesting but I thought it was ________________ too long.
3 As soon as you have any news, please ________________ me a line.
4 Mrs Davies' car broke down so she had to ________________ to the class for being late.
5 The book was terrible – I really ________________ buying it.
6 My ________________ advisor did a good job in helping me choose my university course.
7 I don't know when we'll be arriving, but I'll ________________ you know as soon as I can.
8 When I confronted her, she ________________ losing the earrings I had lent her.
9 The hotel looked great on the website. But unfortunately, it didn't ________________ up to our expectations.
10 It's such bad news, and I don't know how to ________________ it to him.

/10

GRAMMAR

2 Complete the sentences with the words in the list. There are two extra words.

didn't | had | hadn't | was | wasn't | will | would | wouldn't

1 I feel sick. If only I ________________ eaten so much!
2 Davide said he ________________ seen Haruki the day before.
3 Elena asked Mike if he ________________ be at the football match that afternoon.
4 I'm sure I'd understand if only they ________________ speak so fast.
5 My friend asked me why I ________________ looking so down.
6 She phoned to say that unfortunately, she ________________ be able to attend the meeting.

3 Find mistakes in four of the sentences and correct them.

1 I'd sooner had a quick salad and then go back to work.
2 I wish he doesn't give me so many presents – it was so embarrassing.
3 Nell said the film at the cinema was excellent.
4 They announced that the president would make a speech before tomorrow's ceremony.
5 I'd rather you come round to my house, if that's possible.
6 He accused me to break his camera.

/12

FUNCTIONAL LANGUAGE

4 Choose the correct options.

1 A You'll never *know* / *believe* what Harry said to me.
B What? Did he ask you *to join* / *joining* his band?
2 A I'd *rather* / *prefer* you played that music more quietly.
B Well, I'd *rather* / *prefer* it if you went to your own room.
3 A I'd rather you *didn't* / *don't* hang around in the house all day.
B But I don't want to go out! I'd prefer *to sit* / *I sat* and watch TV here.
4 A Have you *heard* / *seen* about Jack's accident?
B Yes, I have, but do you *hear* / *know* what really happened?

/8

MY SCORE /30

22–30 | 10–21 | 0–9

11 SHOOT FOR THE STARS

Get THINKING

Watch the video and think: why are people so fascinated by space?

OBJECTIVES

FUNCTIONS: sympathising about past situations

GRAMMAR: speculating (past, present and future); cause and effect linkers

VOCABULARY: space idioms; adjectives commonly used to describe films

A

B

READING

1 **What can you see in the photos? What do you know about Mars?**

2 SPEAKING **Work in pairs and discuss the questions.**

1 Do you think humans will land on Mars in the next 30 years?
2 Why might a Mars landing be a good thing, and why might it be a bad thing?

3 **Read the article quickly. Does it mention any of your opinions? Do you agree with the opinions in the article?**

4 11.01 **Read and listen to the article again and answer the questions.**

1 Why would 2018 have been a good year to try and get to Mars?
2 Why will any Mars expedition probably involve more than one country?
3 How is Falcon 9 different from other rockets?
4 What could be done to help stop crew members getting bored?
5 How is the Hi-Seas project helping research?
6 What ideas are being explored to help overcome the problem of radiation?
7 What is cross-contamination and how might it affect Mars?
8 Why should we think twice before trying to inhabit Mars?

5 SPEAKING **Work in pairs and discuss the questions.**

1 If it became possible for humans to travel to or live on Mars, would you want to go?
2 If you were living on Mars, what would you miss the most about Earth?

A MISSION TO **MARS**

Back in 2001, Dennis Tito made a name for himself by becoming the first ever space tourist. Twelve years later, he launched his Mars Project with the idea of sending a couple on a flight around Mars. It never happened. The technology wasn't ready. 2018 may have been our best chance to get to Mars from Earth for some time, as the two planets were at their closest, meaning the 35-million-mile journey might have taken as little as 200 days. Huge advances in science over recent years have meant that interest in reaching our closest planetary neighbour is at an all-time high, and we might not have to wait too long before it becomes a reality. The next time the two planets will come closer again is in 2033. The race for Mars is on. However, any space project wishing to touch down on the red planet will first have to overcome three major problems.

Firstly, there is the expense. Current estimates for a return journey range from $100 billion to as much as $500 billion. Clearly this is a lot of money for any one government to find, which means a mission to Mars is certain to be an international collaboration. One way of bringing the cost down, is to work on developing reusable rockets. SpaceX, one of the companies at the forefront of space exploration, believe their Falcon 9, which has already successfully been launched and landed, might be the answer to this.

Another problem that needs overcoming is the psychological effects of such an ambitious journey on the astronauts. Medical experts are worried that the long time spent in a confined space can't be beneficial to the mental health of the crew. They advise that space crafts should be fitted with a wide range of activities to keep the astronauts busy. There is also the question of how well the astronauts will cope with the desert-like Martian landscape. The Hi-Seas project aims to help prepare for this and sees would-be astronauts spending up to eight months in isolation on the side of a Hawaiian volcano.

The final problem is perhaps the most serious. A journey to Mars is bound to expose crew members to extremely high levels of radiation, which is highly likely to lead to a number of illnesses. Ideas being worked on to fight this include the development of protective covering and the possibility of faster rockets to cut down journey time.

Although human exploration of Mars seems certain at some future date, there are those who say there are several reasons why this might not be such a good idea. Perhaps the greatest fear is that of cross-contamination: no matter how sterile the spaceships landing on Mars might be, the astronauts walking out on to the surface will bring with them millions of Earth microbes and the effect of these on any potential Martian ecosystem may well be disastrous. Perhaps we'd be better off concentrating on looking after the world we currently have, so that there will never be any need to find an alternative home.

Train to THINK

Spotting flawed arguments

There are many different ways in which people can try to convince you that something is true without using actual evidence. Here are three common ways.

A The ignorance argument: *Not being able to disprove something doesn't mean it's true. Something is only true if there is evidence for it.*

B Judging by emotions: *Just because someone has strong emotions doesn't always mean that what they say is true. Think carefully before you are persuaded by their argument.*

C Quoting an authority: *Sometimes an expert or their work is quoted and this is used as evidence that something is true. But these people can make mistakes, too. They're not always right. Or their work could be taken out of context. Be careful – 'experts' are often used in advertising to try to sell things to you!*

6 Read the quotations and match them with explanations A–C.

1 I saw this scientist on TV. He says that we should eat more fatty foods. ☐

2 I really dislike politicians and never believe anything they say. ☐

3 **A** I didn't take it. I wasn't even there.
  B You must have taken it if you were there on your own. ☐

7 SPEAKING **Work in pairs. For each of the statements below, create three different flawed arguments (A, B and C) to support it.**

1 Spiders make good pets.

2 Tall people are healthier.

3 Money always brings unhappiness.

The man in the pet shop says I should buy a tarantula from him because they are really easy to look after.

GRAMMAR

Grammar video ▶29

Speculating (past, present and future)

1 Look back at the article on page 103 and complete the sentences with the words from the list. Then complete the rule.

bound to | can't be | certain to | highly likely | may have | might be | might not have to

1 2018 __________ been our best chance to get Mars for some time.
2 We __________ wait too long before it becomes a reality.
3 A mission to Mars is __________ be an international collaboration.
4 SpaceX ... believe their Falcon 9 __________ the answer to this.
5 ... the long time spent in a confined space __________ beneficial to the mental health of the crew.
6 A journey to Mars is __________ expose crew members to extremely high levels of radiation.
7 ... radiation which is __________ to lead to a number of illnesses.

RULE: To speculate we often use the modal verbs *might, may, could, must* and *can't*.

- *might, may* and [8] __________ refer to possibility.
- [9] __________ refers to a perceived impossibility.
- [10] __________ refers to a perceived certainty.

When we refer to past events, the modals are followed by [11] __________ + past participle.

When we refer to present or future events the modals are followed by [12] __________.

We can also use *be + bound to* / [13] __________ *to / likely to* to speculate about past, present and future events.

- *be + bound to / certain to* express greater certainty than *be likely to*.

2 Choose the correct answers.

1 They *must / can't* have got lost. Otherwise they'd be here by now.
2 They *might / can't* have got lost. They know the way.
3 They *might / must* have got lost. Or maybe they left home late.
4 Lea is *certain to / can't* know what to do. She always has good advice.
5 Bram *must / is bound to* be late. He always is.
6 It is *likely / certain* to rain today. You might need an umbrella.
7 You *must / can't* be hungry. You haven't eaten all day.
8 You *can't / might* be hungry. You've just eaten.

3 SPEAKING **How possible do you think these things are? Discuss with a partner and put them in order of probability.**

- humans landing on Mars in the next ten years
- a world free of pollution
- you going on holiday abroad this year

→ workbook page 100

PRONUNCIATION

Stress on modal verbs for speculation

Go to page 121.

FUNCTIONS

Sympathising about past situations

4 Match the sentences and the replies.

1 Alex didn't pass his driving test. ☐
2 So when I went to check in, I realised I'd left my passport at home. ☐
3 The shop had already closed when they got there. ☐
4 Dad crashed Mum's car yesterday. ☐

a Oh, dear. She can't have been happy about that.
b What a shame. They must have been disappointed.
c Poor him. He must have been upset.
d How terrible. You must have been so annoyed.

5 Put the conversation in order.

☐ **Amy** I wasn't. I didn't even have a book with me.
1 **Amy** You won't believe what happened to me on my way home.
☐ **Amy** I didn't get home until midnight. My mum was waiting up for me.
☐ **Amy** It was. And to make things worse, my phone was out of battery.
☐ **Amy** She was. But of course, I couldn't phone her and let her know.
☐ **Amy** I missed my train and had to wait three hours for the next one.
☐ **Tom** Oh, no. You had to wait for three hours? How terrible. That must have been boring.
☐ **Tom** What? Poor you. You can't have been happy about that.
☐ **Tom** Oh, dear. She must have been worried.
☐ **Tom** What happened?
☐ **Tom** So you must have got home really late.

6 Think of something annoying that happened to you recently. Make notes about what happened.

7 SPEAKING **Work in pairs. Tell each other your stories from Exercise 6 and sympathise.**

LISTENING

8 Look at the photos. What do you think is special about this vehicle?

9 11.04 **Listen to the podcast to check your ideas.**

10 11.04 **Listen again and choose the correct answer, A, B or C.**

1 What happened in the years after Denis Tito became the first space tourist?
   - A Flights were stopped altogether.
   - B There was a mad rush of people going into space.
   - C Not as many people as expected followed his example.

2 How many people can the VSS Unity take into space at one time?
   - A two   B six   C eight

3 How long will space tourists on the VSS Unity spend in space?
   - A around two hours
   - B less than two hours
   - C six days

4 Why is the White Knight Two aircraft needed?
   - A to take the VSS Unity on its 14,000m journey into space and back
   - B to help land the VSS Unity
   - C to get the VSS Unity off the Earth's surface

5 Which of these things can tourists do on board the VSS Unity?
   - A take photos of the wonderful views
   - B help land the plane
   - C enjoy being weightless for a while

6 How many people have already paid for flights into space?
   - A 20   B 200   C 700

11 SPEAKING **Work in pairs and discuss the questions.**

1 Do you think space holidays to the moon will be commonplace one day? Why/why not?
2 If you had the money, would you like to go on a trip like this? Why/why not?
3 What else could you better spend this money on?

VOCABULARY
Space idioms

12 Match sentences 1–6 with follow-up sentences a–f.

1 Jen's been accepted by Cambridge University. ☐
2 You'll like Mike. ☐
3 The special effects in the new *Star Wars* film are amazing. ☐
4 Anyone can boil an egg. ☐
5 We very rarely go to the cinema. ☐
6 He thinks every city he visits is the most perfect place in the world. ☐

a They're *out of this world*.
b *It's not rocket science*.
c Maybe *once in a blue moon*.
d He's very *starry-eyed*.
e She's *over the moon*.
f He's very *down to earth* and easy to get on with.

13 Match the expressions from Exercise 12 with the definitions.

1 really happy
2 normal (not at all pretentious)
3 incredible
4 It's very simple.
5 hardly ever
6 overly romantic / overly optimistic

→ workbook page 102

Top four SPACE FILMS of the 21st century

NASA's InSight's thrilling touchdown on the surface of Mars got me thinking a lot about space. So, with that in mind, I've decided to come up with a list of my four favourite space films of the 21st century so far. It wasn't easy choosing just four (and you might not agree with me), but here they are.

1 ARRIVAL (2016)

Arrival isn't exactly action-packed. Not much happens, but it still leaves you thinking about it for days and days afterwards. It stars Amy Adams as Louise Banks, a linguist who is asked by the American military to try and help them communicate with an alien spaceship. It is one of 12 ships that have landed in various locations around Earth. Because of increased tensions between these countries, Louise must work quickly to decipher the codes the aliens are sending and discover exactly why they are here. It is a memorable film and was considered by many critics to be one of 2016's top films.

2 GRAVITY (2009)

I saw this one in 3D on the big screen and it blew me away. In a word, it's stunning. The shots of outer space are so breathtaking that you spend the whole time thinking you are actually up there yourself. I don't want to give away too much of the plot, but due to a run of incredible bad luck, the astronaut played by Sandra Bullock finds herself all alone in the International Space Station, with little hope of ever getting home. Will she or won't she? Watch and you'll find out. *Gravity*, which also features George Clooney – all too briefly – was a huge box office success, but also a hit with the critics. It won a total of seven Academy Awards.

3 FIRST MAN (2018)

This one differs from my other choices because it's based on a true story. Neil Armstrong is the First Man referred to in the title of this film: the first man on the moon. He is played brilliantly by Ryan Gosling in this biopic of America's most famous astronaut. It's full of fascinating details and things you never knew. It's very moving at times, especially when dealing with the death of Armstrong's young daughter. At times it does get a little sentimental, perhaps as a result of having Steven Spielberg as an executive producer. A must for all space travel fans and highly recommended for everyone else.

4 THE MARTIAN (2015)

I've saved the best till last. Matt Damon plays astronaut Mark Watney, who is part of a space mission to explore Mars. He gets caught up in a huge storm and the rest of his crew, deciding that he must be dead, return home without him. Watney must now somehow survive everything the planet can throw at him and try and find a way of making contact with his base back on Earth. The plot might seem a bit far-fetched, but scientists agree that the film gets a lot right about Mars. The special effects are amazing, and consequently, this film is best seen on the big screen. But even on a small screen, this is easily the best space film of all time.

READING

1 Read the blog quickly. Which film does the writer consider to be the greatest space film of all time?

2 11.05 Read and listen to the blog again. Complete the sentences with the names of the films.

1 ______________________ is about someone faced with an impossible journey.
2 ______________________ has a long-lasting effect on its audience.
3 ______________________ takes place on another planet in our solar system.
4 ______________________ is most likely to make you cry.
5 ______________________ should really be seen at the cinema.
6 ______________________ is about a real person.
7 ______________________ has won a lot of prizes.
8 ______________________ involves someone trying to understand a different language.

3 SPEAKING Work in pairs and discuss the questions.

1 Which of these films have you seen or would you like to see?
2 Which films do you think are missing from the list?
3 Why does the writer refer to these films as space films rather than sci-fi films?
4 What do you think is the best sci-fi film of all time?

GRAMMAR
Cause and effect linkers

4 Complete the sentences. Then look back at the blog to check your answers and complete the rule.

1 ... ______________________ increased tensions between these countries, Louise must work quickly.
2 ... ______________________ a run of incredible bad luck, the astronaut played by Sandra Bullock finds herself all alone.
3 ... it gets a little sentimental, perhaps ______________________ having Steven Spielberg as an executive producer.
4 The special effects are amazing, and ______________________ , this film is best seen on the big screen.

> **RULE:** We use linkers such as *due to*, *as a result of*, *because of* and *consequently* to link actions and their consequences.
> *Due to*, *as a result of* and [5] ______________________ can come at the beginning of a sentence or in the middle between the two clauses. They are followed by the reason for an action or event.
> These linkers are usually followed by a noun phrase.
> *Due to* and *as a result of* are more formal than *because of*.
> [6] ______________________ generally comes at the beginning of a new sentence or clause. It introduces the effect of the cause mentioned in the previous sentence. It is followed by a clause (subject and verb).

5 Complete the second sentence so that it has a similar meaning to the first sentence, using the word in brackets. You must use between two and five words, including the word given.

0 Olivia didn't have time to study for the test. Consequently, she didn't do very well. (because)
Because of lack of time to study, Olivia didn't do well in the test.
1 Paul ate too much. He felt ill. (result)
As a ______________________ too much, Paul felt ill.
2 The weather was bad so the race was cancelled. (due)
The race was cancelled ______________________ .
3 Jack had a bad cold. He didn't go to school. (of)
Jack didn't go to school ______________________ cold.
4 The police got some information and arrested the man. (result)
The man was arrested ______________________ information given to the police.
5 No one was interested so the concert was cancelled. (due)
The concert was cancelled ______________________ lack of interest.

→ workbook page 101

VOCABULARY
Adjectives commonly used to describe films

6 Match the highlighted words from the blog with the definitions below.

1 causing strong feelings ______________________
2 really beautiful ______________________
3 really exciting ______________________
4 overly emotional ______________________
5 difficult to believe ______________________
6 full of action ______________________
7 really exciting and really beautiful ______________________
8 something you won't forget ______________________

7 Choose the correct word to complete each sentence.

1 The ending of the film was really *thrilling* / *sentimental*. I was on the edge of my seat.
2 I was surprised that the ending of the film was so *stunning* / *sentimental*. It was a horror film, after all.
3 It's a *moving* / *far-fetched* film. I was close to tears at the end.
4 It's full of explosions and fights and car chases. It's a really *action-packed* / *moving* film.
5 I know it was a fantasy film, but for me the story was so *far-fetched* / *memorable* that it just seemed ridiculous.
6 The characters were a bit dull, but the costumes were *thrilling* / *stunning*.
7 It's a really *sentimental* / *memorable* film. I'm sure I'll be thinking about it for days.
8 The opening scenes of the film are *action-packed* / *breathtaking*. They're absolutely beautiful.

8 SPEAKING **Work in pairs. Think of a film as an example for each of the sentences in Exercise 7.**

→ workbook page 102

SPEAKING

9 Work in pairs. Choose one of the categories below and think of four films for it. As you discuss your choices, use the adjectives in Exercise 6 to help you describe your films and agree on your final list.

- the four greatest comedies
- the four greatest romantic films
- the four greatest action films
- the four greatest horror films

THINK

Being an astronaut

Culture

1 Scan the text to find the answers to these questions.

1 What countries are engaged in space exploration these days?
2 What is the future of the ISS?

2 11.06 **Read and listen to the text to check your answers.**

A multinational enterprise

Somewhere up there in the skies, 400 km above your head, a huge metallic structure the size of an American football pitch is orbiting the Earth every hour and a half, as it travels at speeds of up to 28,000 km/h. Inside, you will find several sleeping areas, two bathrooms, a gym and a 360° window offering some of the most spectacular views you can imagine. You will also find people!

It's the International Space Station (or ISS for short) and as its name suggests, it truly is the result of a huge collaboration between many different countries. The main financial contributors are the US, Russia, Canada, Europe and Japan. Although it is constantly being added to and adapted, the main construction of it was completed between 1998 and 2011. It was taken up into space piece by piece, using NASA's space shuttle to transport most of the larger pieces. Once up there, these pieces were assembled by robots and astronauts.

Since November 2nd 2000, it has been called home by 230 astronauts from 18 different countries. The majority (145) have been from the US, with Russia sending the second most (46). Other countries that have sent astronauts include Italy, Japan, Brazil, Malaysia and South Africa.

Although English is the official language of the Space Station, astronauts are also expected to learn Russian, as technical commands are given in that language. This has led to the creation of 'Runglish' – a mixture of the two – that many of the astronauts use to socialise in their everyday life on board the station.

These days, the ISS generally has a crew of three to six people living on it. Their journey begins on board a Russian Soyuz spaceship, which transports them from Earth to the station where they spend on average six months before returning home. In case of emergency, they can always evacuate the station using one of the two Soyuz spaceships that are docked to the ISS.

During their time there, crew members have a number of different responsibilities. One of the main reasons they are there is to conduct scientific experiments in space. These range from growing plants, to observing the effect of life in space on the human body, in order to understand the challenges humans will face if they want to explore further into the solar system. They also test products such as 3D printers and coffee makers to see how they perform in zero gravity. But the astronauts are also responsible for making sure the ISS is in full working order and they will often need to make repairs which might involve spacewalks to access the exterior of the station. They also put aside two hours each day for exercise and to make sure they are taking care of themselves.

But the ISS might well not be there forever. At the moment, there are plans to keep it in operation until at least 2024 and possibly until 2028, but after that, its future is not so certain. It might be taken out of orbit permanently or broken up into parts to be used on future space stations. But whatever happens to it, let's hope the spirit of international co-operation will continue as mankind explores further and further into space.

3 Read the article again and answer the questions.

1 How big is the ISS?
2 How was it built?
3 What is Runglish? When is it used?
4 How do astronauts get to the ISS?
5 What kinds of experiments do astronauts do on the ISS?
6 Why might an astronaut need to make a spacewalk?

4 VOCABULARY **Match the highlighted words in the article with the definitions.**

1 a partnership/working together
2 to leave somewhere in a hurry (usually because of danger)
3 the force that keeps us on the ground
4 working
5 circling around an object
6 attached to
7 the outside of a building/structure
8 put together

5 SPEAKING **Work in pairs and discuss the questions.**

1 Would you like to spend time in a space station if it was possible?
2 What experiment would you like to conduct most?
3 What do you think would be the most difficult aspect of living on the ISS?

WRITING
A report

1 INPUT **Read the report. What problem does it report and what solution does it suggest?**

1 The aim of this report is to discuss a problem recently encountered during the Admiral 9 mission to the International Space Station and to make suggestions about what can be done to prevent this happening in the future.

2 On 3 September this year, commander Captain Jade Logan reported a serious incident of computer malfunction in the dining quarters of the International Space Station. On further inspection, it appeared that the computer had stopped working due to it being covered in a thick orange liquid. Logan questioned members of her team only to discover that the problem had occurred when engineer Ian Coyne's carrot soup had leaked from its container and found its way to the computing area.

3 Although the crew were able to run the back-up computer, the incident has raised serious concerns about dining habits. Consequently, while a more detailed report is being prepared, we suggest an immediate ban on all liquid food aboard the Space Station until safer procedures can be introduced.

2 ANALYSE **Match the paragraphs with their main function. There are two extra functions.**

☐ say who is responsible
☐ a brief description of what the report is about
☐ suggestions for changes
☐ talk about the cost of making changes
☐ an outline of the problem

3 **Rewrite the sentences from the report, replacing the underlined words with the words in brackets.**

The computer had stopped working due to it being covered in a thick orange liquid.

1 (as a result of)
2 (because of)

Although the crew were able to run the back-up computer, the incident has raised serious concerns about dining habits.

3 (however)
4 (despite)

4 PLAN **Read through the situation below and make notes.**

Last Friday, there was a school trip to the space museum. The coach was supposed to leave at 9 am, but didn't leave until 10 am because five students were late. As a consequence, the group had an hour less to spend at the museum.

Problem: ____________________

Solution: ____________________

5 PRODUCE **Write a report about the problem with the school trip (200–250 words). Remember to do these things:**

- say what the report is about
- outline the problem
- suggest a solution

12 OFF THE BEATEN TRACK

Get THINKING

Watch the video and think:
how important is tourism where you live?

OBJECTIVES

FUNCTIONS:
speaking persuasively

GRAMMAR:
passive report structures; the passive: verbs with two objects

VOCABULARY:
geographical features; verb + noun collocations

A

C

B

D

READING

1 **Look at the photos. What do they show? In which parts of the world can they be found? Which do you think don't exist anymore?**

2 **Read the article quickly to check your ideas.**

3 12.01 **Read and listen to the article again. Answer the questions.**

1 What is happening to many beautiful and ancient destinations around the world?
2 What was the Chacaltaya Glacier's claim to fame?
3 What caused the Chacaltaya Glacier to disappear so quickly?
4 What was important about Sir Alfred Maudslay's trip to Tikal?
5 What is happening to the forests around the Mayan ruins of Tikal?
6 What might help protect the Nazca Lines?
7 What part does tourism play in the destruction of the Nazca Lines?
8 Why is the Dead Sea shrinking so rapidly?

4 SPEAKING **Work in pairs and discuss the questions.**

1 What can be done to stop these places and other amazing places from disappearing?
2 Can you think of any places in your own country which are in danger of disappearing?
3 Which of the places in the article would you most like to visit? Why? Do you think you should?
4 Do you think there are other places in the world where tourism should be limited?

Saving great discoveries!

Many places discovered by explorers in past centuries are now in danger of disappearing, and many have already disappeared. Sadly, forests, lakes, glaciers and ancient ruins are gradually being destroyed by global warming and man-made disasters. What can we do to save them?

The Chacaltaya Glacier

5,300 m up in the Andes
STATUS: disappeared

The Chacaltaya Glacier in the Andes was once the highest ski run in the world. The summit was in fact higher than the base camp at Mount Everest.

The glacier, which is believed to be 18,000 years old, was 0.22 km^2 in area in 1940. It shrank to 0.08 km^2 in 1996, before finally disappearing completely in 2005. So why did it disappear? The answer is climate change. Scientists predicted that it would disappear in 2015. In fact, it melted a lot more quickly.

Climate change is destroying other glaciers, too. In Iceland, it is believed scientists have found a solution. They inject carbon dioxide into rock. The carbon dioxide gas then turns to rock, too. This helps to stop temperatures rising and the ice melting.

The Mirador Basin and Tikal National Park

Forest home to Mayan ruins in Guatemala
STATUS: losing 100,000 acres of forest a year

The Mirador Basin and Tikal National Park in Guatemala are home to the amazing pyramids and ruins of the Mayan civilization. In 1881, the explorer Sir Alfred Maudslay took the first photos of the ancient Mayan city.

Nowadays, the area is said to be losing 100,000 acres of forest a year. It's being burnt for farms. One solution to this is to ask villagers to help protect the land.

The Nazca Lines

Ancient chalk drawings in Peru
STATUS: in danger of disappearing

The Peruvian archaeologist Toribio Mejia Xesspe was the first to study the Nazca Lines. He discovered them while he was exploring the area, in 1927. These ancient chalk drawings show more than a hundred different figures, including flowers, animals and humans, and are the oldest of their kind in the world. The largest figures stretch more than 200 metres across. It is believed that they date back to a time between 500 BCE and 500 CE.

In recent years, however, tourism has brought litter and vandalism. To help protect the Nazca lines, barriers could be built on the road that runs through them. This would protect the drawings from cars and trucks which sometimes drive onto them.

The Dead Sea

A salt-water lake in Jordan
STATUS: 24 metres shallower than 40 years ago

The Dead Sea Scrolls are very important pieces of writing discovered in the area around the Dead Sea. Sadly, the Dead Sea has decreased in size by a third in the past 40–45 years, and it is known to have sunk over 24 metres since the 1980s. If countries around the sea continue to use water from the River Jordan, it is thought that the sea will not exist in 50 years' time. Action must be taken now to change the way people use the water from the River Jordan so that we can save this beautiful salt lake.

Train to THINK

Exploring hidden messages

People don't always say what they mean. For example, imagine you show a short story you've written to a friend and ask for their opinion. What do you think when they tell you, 'I thought the beginning was great.'? Was the beginning really good, or are they trying to hide the fact that they didn't really like the rest of it? People do this for a number of reasons: they don't want to be rude; they're not brave enough to tell the truth; or they don't really have an opinion.

5 **Look at what these people have said. What do you think they might really be hiding?**

1 That's an interesting jumper you're wearing.
2 There's an earlier train you could catch, if you want.
3 Joe always has a lot to say for himself.
4 Your homework reminded me a lot of Simon's.

6 SPEAKING **Work in pairs. Read the situations. What could you say without being too direct?**

1 Your dad has cooked something new that you really don't like.
2 Your best friend asks you what you think about their new haircut. You think it's awful.
3 Your aunt's annoying dog keeps barking.

GRAMMAR
Passive report structures

1 **Find and <u>underline</u> the sentences in the article which mean the same as 1–5. Then complete the rule with *written, past* or *present*.**

1 People believe that they were drawn 1,500 to 2,500 years ago.
2 People think that the sea will disappear completely in the next 50 years.
3 Experts believe that this ancient glacier is thousands of years old.
4 We know that the Dead Sea has sunk over 24 metres since the 1980s.
5 People say that the area is losing thousands of acres of forest every year.

> **RULE:** An example of a passive report structure is:
> *Thousands of caves **are thought to exist** in China.*
> We can also say:
> ***It is thought** that thousands of caves exist in China.*
> These structures use reporting verbs like *say, think, believe, know* and *consider*.
> If we use a passive report structure to talk about beliefs or knowledge of [6]________________ actions, we use the correct form of *be* + past participle of the reporting verb + *to* + infinitive:
> *She **is said to be** one of the greatest explorers of all time.*
> ***It is said** that she is one of the greatest explorers of all time.*
> If we use a passive report structure to talk about beliefs or knowledge of [7]________________ actions, we use the correct form of *be* + past participle of the reporting verb + *to* + *have* + past participle:
> *Many people **are known to have died** on the expedition.*
> Passive report structures are more often used in [8]________________ or more formal language, e.g. newspaper reports.

2 **Rewrite the following sentences using passive report structures.**

0 Experts know that Death Valley is the hottest place on Earth. Death Valley *is known to be the hottest place on Earth*.
1 We believe that the ice in Antarctica is disappearing.
The ice in Antarctica ________________.
2 People say that this cave is 500 metres deep.
This cave ________________
3 Experts think that most fish in the deep ocean are blind.
Most fish ________________.
4 We know that the Sahara Desert contained water only 5,000 years ago.
The Sahara Desert ________________.
5 Experts believe that some deep-sea creatures have existed for millions of years.
Some deep-sea creatures ________________.

→ workbook page 108

VOCABULARY
Geographical features

3 **Match the words with the photos. Write 1–8 in the boxes.**

1 bay | 2 canyon | 3 dune
4 glacier | 5 mountain range
6 reef | 7 volcano | 8 waterfall

A

E

B

F

C

G

D

H

4 **Complete each sentence with a word from Exercise 3.**

1 There's often snow on the top of a very high ________________.
2 It can be difficult to run up a ________________ because it's all sand.
3 When water goes over the edge of a ________________, it often looks white.
4 A ________________ can be dangerous for ships, because it's just below the surface of the sea.
5 If a ________________ is active, it sometimes erupts and can be very dangerous.
6 It can take a very long time for a ________________ to move even as little as ten centimetres.
7 A ________________ is sometimes a good place for ships to stop, because it's protected by land on three sides.
8 There's usually a river at the bottom of a ________________.

5 SPEAKING **Work in pairs. You have three minutes to think of as many famous examples of the features in Exercise 3 as you can. Then compare your ideas with another pair.**

→ workbook page 110

LISTENING

6 Match the photos and the names. Write 1–4 in the boxes.

1 giant rat | 2 gibbon | 3 pocket shark | 4 rainfrog

A

B

C

D

7 Which of the creatures do you think is named after a *Star Wars* character? Why?

8 12.02 Listen to someone giving a talk about animal species. What is true about all of the creatures?

9 12.02 Listen again and answer the questions.

1 Why is the tiny shark called a pocket shark?
2 When was the last time a new rat species was found in the South Pacific?
3 Which three things are different about Skywalker gibbons?
4 What makes this frog eye-catching?
5 What can we do to protect these animals?

FUNCTIONS

Speaking persuasively

10 12.03 Listen again to the end of the talk. Complete the text.

'... all these animals are [1]________________ . Their habitat, that is the places where they live, is being destroyed rapidly, and it is [2]________________ who are doing this. If we [3]________________ now, to stop habitats being destroyed, many animals will disappear and future generations will only see them in books. I think it's [4]________________ for humans to find ways to live well and without harming other living creatures, [5]________________ ?

11 In the extract in Exercise 10, underline these things.

1 adjectives and adverbs used to make a point strongly
2 a question tag
3 a conditional clause to show urgency

12 WRITING Write two or three sentences for a speech in which someone wants to persuade listeners about these things.

1 Traffic has to be reduced in a town.
2 Having a new supermarket in a town is a bad idea.
3 A leisure centre is needed in a town.

PRONUNCIATION
Linking: intrusive /r/ Go to page 121.

TH!NK values

Human activity and the natural world

13 Read what the speaker says at the end of the talk. Then think about the questions. Make notes.

... forests are being turned into fields to grow food, and trees are being cut down to get wood, and rivers are being used by more and more boats, and so these animals find it harder and harder to live.

1 Can you give any real-life examples of what she's describing?
2 What other problems can human activity cause? (not just problems for animals)
3 Do you think there might be problems if people explore the deep ocean? What kind of problems?

14 SPEAKING Work in pairs or small groups.

1 Use your notes from Exercise 13. Decide on the question you are most interested in.
2 Together, prepare a two-minute presentation entitled 'Human activity and the natural world'.
3 Give your presentation to the class.

EXPLORERS

Almost every country on our planet has been explored and mapped and all of these have roads, railways and lines of communication. So it can be hard for us to imagine the people who went there without all the infrastructure that we now take for granted.

This series celebrates the men and women who opened the world up and risked their lives to protect the people and environments they discovered along the way. This week, we profile a man not well-known outside his own country and continent – Cândido Rondon.

A FRIEND TO NATIVE PEOPLE CÂNDIDO RONDON

In 1865, in a small village in the state of Mato Grosso, Brazil, a boy was born. His father was of Portuguese ancestry and his mother was a native Brazilian. Who could have known that his origins would play such a big part in helping to connect so many cultures in very real and visible ways?

He decided to join the army as an engineer and when he was only 25, he was involved in the building of a road from Rio de Janeiro to Cuiabá, a journey that previously could only be made by boat. He was later given the monumental task of placing telegraph lines from Brazil to Bolivia and Peru. This was a difficult job through rough and unexplored terrain, so it required a skilled engineer. Rondon opened paths through uncharted territory, and he came into contact with the Bororo, a tribe he had family connections with on his mother's side. Rondon established a friendly and respectful relationship with the Bororo people, and the telegraph lines were completed with their help.

Next, Rondon was given the job of extending the telegraph system from Mato Grosso to the Amazon. This time he came across and made friends with the Nambikwara, previously thought of as a timid but hostile tribe. Rondon got to know many tribes during his expeditions, and he was a great friend to them. He was disturbed and ashamed to learn about the terrible way that they were often treated by outsiders. He fought long and hard to protect them and their right to follow their own beliefs, traditions and customs.

However, some people still considered him an outsider. During his expeditions in Amazonia, Rondon was attacked several times, and once he was wounded by an arrow. Other members of the expedition wanted to take revenge on the native people who had attacked them, but Rondon said, 'Die if necessary, but never kill.' Years later, Rondon set up Brazil's Indian Protection Service, an agency to safeguard the interests and support the cultures of native peoples. Rondon's famous words became its motto.

Rondon died in 1958 and is remembered as a hero in Brazil. A state in Brazil (Rondônia) was named after him, as well as the airport in Cuiabá and several roads.

▶ ***Next week: Abel Tasman***

READING

1 SPEAKING **Work in pairs. Discuss what you know about when the main roads, railways and telephone lines were built in your country. Think about these things:**

1. how and when the main roads (and/or railways) were built, and by whom
2. how communications, such as telephone lines, started, and when
3. any difficulties people had when building the roads, telephone lines, etc.

2 **Look at the title of the article and the pictures. What do you think Rondon achieved? Read the article quickly to check.**

3 12.06 **Read and listen to the article again. Mark the sentences T (true), F (false) or DS (doesn't say). Then correct the false sentences.**

1. Cândido Rondon was half Portuguese and half Brazilian. ☐
2. Rondon was considered a good engineer. ☐
3. The Nambikwara were not friendly to Rondon. ☐
4. Rondon was upset by the way strangers treated the tribes. ☐
5. Rondon's motto came from one of the tribes. ☐
6. Many people in Brazil still appreciate what Rondon did for the country. ☐

4 SPEAKING **Work in pairs and discuss the questions.**

1. What do you understand by Rondon's motto, 'Die if necessary, but never kill.'?
2. What places in your country are named after famous people?
3. Who would you name an airport after in your country?

GRAMMAR

Grammar video ▶32

The passive: verbs with two objects

5 Check which of these three sentences is in the article on page 114. Then complete the rule with *person*, *direct* and *indirect*.

1 They gave Rondon the job of extending the telegraph system.
2 The job of extending the telegraph system was given to Rondon.
3 Rondon was given the job of extending the telegraph system.

> **RULE:** Some verbs (like *give, offer, ask, promise, read, show, write, buy*, etc.) can be followed by two objects (a person and a thing).
> 1 Verb + indirect object + direct object:
> *The teacher read the children a story.*
> 2 Verb + direct object + indirect object:
> *The teacher read a story to the children.*
> There are also two ways of making the passive construction:
> 1 *The **children** were read a story.*
> ([4]_______________ object as subject)
> 2 *A **story** was read to the children.*
> ([5]_______________ object as subject)
> It is more usual to have the [6]_______________ as the subject of the passive construction, not the object.

6 In each pair of sentences, tick (✓) the one that is more usual.

1 A A lot of money was paid to her. ☐
B She was paid a lot of money. ☐
2 A I was told a lie. ☐
B A lie was told to me. ☐
3 A We were promised a big party. ☐
B A big party was promised to us. ☐
4 A I was bought a new pair of shoes. ☐
B A new pair of shoes was bought for me. ☐

7 Rewrite the sentences using the passive. Use the person as subject.

0 They told me a secret.
I was told a secret.
1 They offered my mum a job.
2 People owed my dad a lot of money.
3 They gave him some medicine.
4 Someone promised us a week's holiday.
5 Someone showed me the right way to do it.

→ workbook page 109

VOCABULARY

Verb + noun collocations

8 Complete the sentences about the article on page 114 with the correct verbs.

1 Rondon _______________ friends with the Nambikwara tribe.
2 Before that, the journey could only be _______________ by river transport.
3 They wanted to _______________ revenge on the native people.
4 Who could have known that his origins would _______________ such a big part in helping to connect so many cultures?

9 Complete the table with nouns from the list to make collocations. Some nouns can go into more than one column.

> advantage | advice | amends | a complaint | a deal
> a decision | an effort | an exam | an example
> exercise | a favour | the fool | friends | fun of someone
> good money | an interview | a joke | a journey
> a part | a photo | progress | research | a role
> a speech | a test | a wish

make	take	play	do	give

10 Complete the story with the correct form of the verbs in Exercise 9.

When I got to the small jungle town, I [0]*made* friends with some of the locals and told them that I wanted to [1]_______________ a journey up the river. They thought I was mad! One of them [2]_______________ me some advice – he said, 'Don't go! It's dangerous.' At first, I thought he was [3]_______________ fun of me, but then he [4]_______________ me some examples of the dangers I would face.

But I had [5]_______________ my decision – I wanted to explore. I had [6]_______________ some research about the diseases I might catch and I had [7]_______________ some medical tests to make sure I was in good health. I had worked for years and [8]_______________ a lot of money, so I [9]_______________ a deal with three of the men to come with me.

I needed to leave soon, to [10]_______________ advantage of the good weather and to [11]_______________ as much progress as I could before the rains began. So, the next morning, we met at the port. I put my phone in my pocket (I could use it to [12]_______________ photos) and got into the small boat. I looked at the river – would I make it?

11 WRITING Work in pairs. Write the next paragraph of the story in Exercise 10. Try and include some more collocations from Exercise 9.

→ workbook page 110

Literature

1 **Look at the photo and read the introduction to the extract. Do you think you would like to read the book?**

2 **Read the extract quickly and choose the best ending for the statement.**

The narrator feels worried about …

1 what will happen when the sun comes up.
2 the noise of drums that he can hear.
3 the animals in the jungle around them.

The Lost World by Arthur Conan Doyle (1912)

Professor George Challenger and his friend Lord John Roxton, together with a reporter and some local guides (one of whom is called Gomez), travel up the Amazon River to find a plateau. Challenger claims he has visited the plateau before, and that there are prehistoric creatures living there. Also with them is another professor who dislikes Challenger and doesn't believe his claims. The reporter narrates the story.

The very next day we did actually make our start upon this remarkable expedition. We found that all our possessions fitted very easily into the two canoes, and we divided our personnel, six in each, taking the obvious precaution, in the interests of peace, of putting one professor into each canoe. […]

At dawn and at sunset the monkeys screamed together and the parrots started making their high-pitched noise, but during the hot hours of the day only the loud noise of insects, like the beat of a distant surf, filled the ear, while nothing moved amongst the solemn views of huge tree-trunks, fading away into the darkness which held us in. Once some creature, an ant-eater or a bear, walked clumsily amid the shadows. It was the only sign of life which I had seen in this great Amazonian forest.

And yet there were indications that even human life itself was not far from us in those mysterious dark corners.

On the third day out, we were aware of a strange, deep, rhythmic beat in the air, coming and going on-and-off throughout the morning. The two boats were moving within a few yards of each other when we first heard it, and our guides remained motionless, as if they had been turned to bronze, listening intently with expressions of terror upon their faces.

'What is it, then?' I asked.

'Drums,' said Lord John, carelessly, 'war drums. I have heard them before.'

'Yes, sir, war drums,' said Gomez. 'Native people, aggressive, not friendly; they watch us every mile of the way; kill us if they can.'

'How can they watch us?' I asked, gazing into the dark. Gomez shrugged his broad shoulders.

'The native people know. They have their own way. They watch us. They talk the drum talk to each other. Kill us if they can.'

By the afternoon of that day – my pocket diary shows me that it was Tuesday, August 18th – at least six or seven drums were beating from various points. Sometimes they beat quickly, sometimes slowly, sometimes in obvious question and answer, one far to the east breaking out in a high-pitched beat, and being followed after a pause by a deep roll from the north. There was something incredibly nerve-shaking and threatening in that constant noise, which seemed to shape itself into the words that Gomez used and endlessly repeated them: 'We will kill you if we can. We will kill you if we can.' No one ever moved in the silent woods. All the peace of quiet nature lay in that dark curtain of vegetation, but away from behind, there always came the one message from our fellow-man: 'We will kill you if we can,' said the men in the east. 'We will kill you if we can,' said the men in the north. […]

That night we tied our canoes with heavy stones for anchors in the centre of the stream, and made every preparation for a possible attack. Nothing came, however, and with the dawn we pushed upon our way, the drum-beating dying out behind us.

Adapted from *The Lost World* by Arthur Conan Doyle

3 12.07 **Read and listen to the extract again. Mark the sentences T (true) or F (false). Then correct the false sentences.**

1 There was not enough room for both professors to sit together. ☐
2 The noise of the insects sounded like the sea. ☐
3 They saw some wild animals hiding amongst the trees. ☐
4 The guides were terrified when they heard the drums. ☐
5 The violent attack came at dawn. ☐

4 Match the highlighted words in the extract with the definitions.

1 never changing, always the same
2 not ordinary, amazing
3 very serious and a little sad
4 signs
5 difficult to believe
6 decreasing to nothing
7 stop existing
8 fierce and eager (wanting) to fight

5 SPEAKING **Work in pairs and discuss the questions.**

1 What about this text tells you it was written more than 100 years ago? Give reasons.
2 Which attitudes of the narrator are outdated today?

WRITING
A short biography

1 INPUT **Read Joel's biography of Oliver Tambo and answer the questions.**

1 What did Tambo study during his life?
2 Where did he live, apart from in South Africa?
3 Why did he give the ANC presidency to Nelson Mandela?

2 ANALYSE **Which paragraph is which? Write letters in the boxes in the text.**

A Conclusion
B Early life
C Introduction to the person
D Main achievements

3 PLAN **You're going to write a short biography.**

1 Think of something in your country (e.g. a street, an airport, a square) that has the name of a famous person.
2 Make notes about the person's life. Do research on the internet if you need to.
3 Decide which information is most important to include in a biography.

4 PRODUCE **Now write your biography (200–250 words).**

- Make sure that you include information that makes it clear why the place was named after the person.
- Follow the structure of the biography about Tambo.

☐ Johannesburg is my home city, and the international airport here is called O. R. Tambo airport. It is named after Oliver Tambo, who not many people know much about. Almost everyone has heard of Nelson Mandela, but Tambo is not as well known around the world.

☐ Oliver Reginald Tambo (everyone knew him as O. R.) was born in 1917 in an area of South Africa now known as the Eastern Cape. As a young man he studied education and for a while, he was a teacher. Later, he gave up teaching to study law, and in 1952 he joined Nelson Mandela's law firm.

☐ These were the years of apartheid in South Africa. Tambo, like Mandela, was part of the African National Congress (ANC), which was an illegal organisation at that time. Mandela was sent to prison on Robben Island and Tambo left the country – he lived at different times in Zambia and in London. He was the 'president in exile' of the ANC and worked very hard to get support from other countries in the struggle to end apartheid.

☐ He went back to South Africa in 1990, when the ANC became legal. But he had a stroke and could not work any longer, so he passed the presidency of the ANC to Mandela. Tambo died in 1993, before he could see the first black government of his country. In 2006, the airport was renamed after him to honour his achievements. And to sum up, I think that this honour rightly recognised the very important role that Tambo played in the development of the country he loved.

LISTENING

Part 2: Sentence completion

→ workbook page 115

1 12.08 **You will hear a woman called Frances Williams talking about her work as an oceanographer. For questions 1–10, complete the sentences with a word or a short phrase.**

Frances believes oceanography is important for dealing with increased [1] ________________ as a result of climate change.

Frances says that marine biologists study the impact of changes in the marine environment on [2] ________________ and animals.

Chemical oceanographers try to find out more about the impact that [3] ________________ has on the quality of the ocean waters.

Some chemical oceanographers try to find resources for new [4] ________________ .

Physical oceanographers focus on movements of the sea, such as how [5] ________________ is moved along coastlines.

Frances' job involves studying how the ocean floor changes as a result of [6] ________________ activity.

Frances says that [7] ________________ of the world's ocean floors have not yet been explored.

Challenger Deep is an area of the ocean that goes down to nearly [8] ________________ .

Frances' research does not confirm the general belief that the ocean's deepest places are [9] ________________ .

Oceanographers have also discovered that there are strong currents that can be compared to extreme [10] ________________ .

READING AND USE OF ENGLISH

Part 4: Key word transformation

→ workbook page 117

2 **For questions 1–6, complete the second sentence so that it has a similar meaning to the first sentence, using the word given. Do not change the word given. You must use between two and five words, including the word given. Here is an example (0).**

Example:

0 Kate has an interest in marine biology.
INTERESTED
Kate ________________ a marine biologist.
Write the missing words in CAPITAL LETTERS.
Kate *IS INTERESTED IN BECOMING* a marine biologist.

1 'Have you got any idea why coral bleaching is happening, Nick?' asked Mia.
IF
Mia asked Nick ________________ for coral bleaching.

2 You can't order this book unless they have an online store.
ONLY
You can ________________ they have an online store.

3 Researchers say that high water temperatures cause coral bleaching.
SAID
High water temperatures ________________ coral bleaching.

4 My friends were in favour of watching the documentary.
IDEA
My friends thought it would be ________________ the documentary.

5 The researcher gave a fascinating talk.
GIVEN
A fascinating talk ________________ the researcher.

6 I'd prefer not to join you.
STAY
I'd ________________ home.

VOCABULARY

1 Complete the sentences with the words in the list. There are four extra words.

action-packed | bonus | breathtaking | do | far-fetched | gave | make
reef | solar | squeezing | solar | star | took | volcano | waterfall

1 My baby cousin drew a picture of me by ________________ toothpaste onto the mirror in the bathroom.
2 Jack has an image of the ________________ system projected on the ceiling of his bedroom.
3 The effect of the fireworks and the music was really ________________ .
4 Flights were disrupted when a ________________ erupted and filled the sky with ash.
5 We climbed up to the top of the ________________ and watched the water pouring down.
6 The water in the bay is always calm because it's protected by a ________________ .
7 Pete's dad gave him some good advice, but I don't think he ________________ it.
8 We weren't expecting good weather on our holiday, so the sunshine was a real ________________ .
9 Christina's presentation is next week, so she needs to ________________ some research on the internet.
10 His excuse for being late was so ________________ that no one believed a word of it.

/10

GRAMMAR

2 Complete the sentences with the phrases in the list. There are two extra phrases.

can't have | consequently | due to | must be | must have | to be | to have | was given

1 Johnny Depp is known ________________ received 50 million US dollars for just one film.
2 Arlo was always eating fast food, and ________________ he put on a lot of weight.
3 Silvia is a terrible singer – she ________________ won the singing competition!
4 London is known ________________ one of the most expensive cities in the world.
5 Hafsa left half an hour ago – she ________________ home by now.
6 Luis ________________ two identical jumpers for his birthday.

3 Find and correct the mistake in each sentence.

1 I'm sure a lot of people have met the new boy. Sofia mustn't be the only one.
2 Only a few people are thought to have survive so long alone in the desert.
3 Oh dear, I'm bound to got this all wrong – I didn't understand the question.
4 My father was brought up by his aunt after his parents were died.
5 Kate Jones is know to have owned three houses, although she has always said that she's very poor.
6 I suppose it's possible – Cara might be at the party last night, but I didn't see her.

/12

FUNCTIONAL LANGUAGE

4 Choose the correct options.

1 A I've lost my phone! I *can* / *must* have left it on the bus.
B Oh *dear* / *shame*, that is a problem.
2 A Last weekend we couldn't find our cat. We thought she *was* / *had been* run over by a car.
B How *shame* / *terrible*! You must have been very worried.
3 A You know, in the past, being left-handed was *believed* / *known* to be unnatural.
B That *mustn't* / *can't* have been easy for left-handed people.
4 A In some countries black cats are *thought* / *known* to be unlucky.
B Yes, but in other countries they are *seen* / *looked* at as bringers of good luck.

/8

MY SCORE /30

22–30 | 10–21 | 0–9

PRONUNCIATION

UNIT 1
Diphthongs: alternative spellings

1 1.02 **Read and listen to the five tongue twisters. Notice the different spellings of the same sounds.**

1 **Simon might**'ve **died** when he **climbed** on the **ice**.
2 **Joe tiptoed alone** through the **snow**.
3 We **stayed** until **late**; when it **rained** we went **straightaway**.
4 When they got **down** from the **mountain** they **found** it was just **out** of **town**.
5 The **boys enjoyed** the **noise** as the water **boiled**.

2 1.03 **Listen, repeat and practise.**

UNIT 2
Phrasal verb stress

1 2.04 **Read and listen to the dialogue below.**

Gillian Moving to France when I was nine was tough. It **turned out** all right, though. I soon made new friends.
Leo How long did it take you to **pick up** French?
Gillian About three months. I **hung out** with my French friends every day, so that helped.
Leo Do you ever **run into** them now?
Gillian **Run into** them? I don't live in France any more!

2 **Choose the correct words.**

Red indicates [1]*primary / secondary* stress. Blue indicates [2]*primary / secondary* stress. In two-part phrasal verbs, primary stress is usually on the [3]*verb / particle* and secondary stress is on the [4]*verb / particle*.

3 2.05 **Listen, repeat and practise.**

UNIT 3
Adding emphasis

1 3.04 **Read and listen to the dialogue.**

Millie Hannah's **such** a good tennis player! Did you see the match yesterday?
Rob Yes! It was **so** exciting!
Millie She didn't win, but she **did** play really well.
Rob It was **such** a pity she lost! She tried **so** hard.
Millie Yes, it was **such** a difficult match.
Rob I know. Anyway, I **do** think she's amazing!

2 3.04 **Listen again. What is the effect of the words in bold?**

3 3.05 **Listen, repeat and practise.**

UNIT 4
Pronouncing words with *gh*

1 4.04 **Read and listen to the forum posts about thinking. What do you notice about the pronunciation of *gh* in the words in bold?**

Paul At first I **thought** it wouldn't be a problem – but now I'm scared I'll only get **through** it with great difficulty.
Sophie Actually, the real problem is the way we've been **brought** up to see problems. Try to stop seeing things as '**right**' or 'wrong'. If you try an idea and other people **laugh** at it, that's their problem, not yours. Anyway, **enough** from me. I hope these ideas help!

2 4.05 **Listen, repeat and practise.**

UNIT 5
The schwa /ə/ sound

1 5.03 **Read and listen to a voicemail message, paying attention to the words in blue. Which sound do they all share?**

Thank you for calling **the** Computer Now Helpline. **To** find out how **to** zip **a** file, upgrade **a** system **or** stream **a** video, press 1. **To** learn how **to** connect **to** wifi, browse **the** internet or post **an** update, press 2. For all other enquiries, press 3.

2 5.04 **Listen, repeat and practise.**

UNIT 6
Linking words with /dʒ/ and /tʃ/

1 6.02 **Read and listen to the dialogue.**

Jack Would you like a cup of tea?
Sally Do you know what? I'd really prefer coffee.
Jack Oh! Did you buy some when you went out?
Sally No. Didn't you?
Jack Don't you remember? I told you we didn't have any coffee!
Sally Do you know what? Tea sounds great!

2 6.03 **Listen, repeat and practise.**

UNIT 7
Intonation: encouraging someone

1 7.05 **Read and listen to the dialogue.**

Becky Hi, Harry! You don't look very happy. What's up?
Harry Well … I just failed my driving test.
Becky Oh! That's too bad … but **don't let it get you down**. Plenty of people fail the first time!
Harry Actually, it's not the first time.
Becky Oh well, **look on the bright side** – you can only get better!
Harry I suppose so … I just feel kind of stupid.
Becky **It'll be all right!** You just need a bit more practice, that's all. **I know you can do it!**

2 7.05 **Draw arrows above the blue phrases to show how Becky's voice goes up and down.**

3 7.06 **Listen, repeat and practise.**

UNIT 8
Weak forms with conditionals

1 8.04 **Read and listen to the dialogue.**

Cora Oh no! I forgot my mum's birthday! I would've remembered if I didn't have all these exams!
Nellie Really, Cora … you could've written it in your diary.
Cora I could've done many things, Nellie. But that's not the point.
Nellie You should've asked your dad to remind you! What are you going to do?

2 8.04 **Listen again and find the word in blue in which the /v/ sound in 've is pronounced. Why do you think this might be?**

3 8.05 **Listen, repeat and practise.**

UNIT 9
Linking: intrusive /w/ and /j/

1 9.02 **Read and listen to the dialogue.**

Ella My parents tell me off all the time. They're always so angry with me!
Ethan Why don't you ask them to explain why they're upset? You might be able to change things …
Ella Why do you always have to have a solution to everything, Ethan? It's so annoying!
Ethan Don't be angry, Ella. I'm only trying to help! You can be annoying, too, you know!

2 9.02 **Listen again and write a *j* or *w* above the underlined words to indicate which intrusive sound you hear.**

3 9.03 **Listen, repeat and practise.**

UNIT 10
Linking: omission of the /h/ sound

1 10.02 **Read and listen to the dialogue.**

Helen Hilary and Hector aren't speaking to each other.
Hugo What happened?
Helen He hurt her feelings. He said he didn't like her new haircut.
Hugo How horrible! Did he mean to upset her?
Helen Of course he didn't!

2 10.02 **Listen again and underline the words in which the letter *h* is silent. Is it silent in stressed or unstressed words?**

3 10.03 **Listen, repeat and practise.**

UNIT 11
Stress on modal verbs for speculation

1 11.02 **Read and listen to the dialogue.**

Gina I just watched a TV show that said the Vikings might have discovered America.
Dale Well … they might have, I suppose.
Gina It said that they may have built some villages in Canada!
Dale It could be true – if they had the boats and technology to get there.
Gina In fact, they may be the greatest explorers in history!
Dale Oh, Gina! That's not very likely, is it?

2 11.02 **Listen again, and colour the box above the word which carries the primary stress.**

3 11.03 **Listen, repeat and practise.**

UNIT 12
Linking: intrusive /r/

1 12.04 **Read and listen to the excerpts from a blog.**

1 We're off on our adventure on Saturday.
2 We're going far away to explore amazing places.
3 We hope to learn more about our incredible Earth.
4 We'll remember our adventure for ever!
5 Join us on our adventure – follow our excellent blog!

2 12.04 **Listen again and find the pairs of words linked with the /r/ sound.**

3 12.05 **Listen, repeat and practise.**

GET IT RIGHT!

UNIT 1

Verb patterns

Learners often use the wrong verb form after certain verbs, using the gerund instead of *to* + infinitive and vice versa.

✓ *I'm looking forward to **going** to the festival.*
✗ *I'm looking forward ~~to go~~ to the festival.*

Which of these sentences are correct and which are incorrect? Rewrite the incorrect ones.

0 Ben was looking forward to climb the cliff.
Ben was looking forward to climbing the cliff.
1 They wanted going sailing but the weather conditions were too extreme.
____
2 I enjoy to wander around outdoor markets when I'm on holiday.
____
3 Zara refused to swing across the river on the rope.
____
4 Do you think you'll manage completing the mountain climb?
____
5 Tim doesn't mind helping out on the mountaineering course at weekends.
____
6 Kate had hoped reaching the glacier by early afternoon but slipped on the ice and broke her leg.
____
7 The children learned building a shelter during the survival course.
____
8 Megan was thrilled when she got her exam results as she'd expected failing.
____

remember, *forget*, *regret*, *try* and *stop*

Learners often use the wrong verb form after the verbs *remember*, *try*, *stop*, *regret* and *forget*, which can all be followed by both the gerund and infinitive but with different meanings.

✓ *I really think you should stop **smoking**.*
✗ *I really think you should ~~stop to smoke~~.*

Choose the correct verb form.

1 Did you remember *buying* / *to buy* some milk?
2 Pablo stopped *getting a drink* / *to get a drink* at a café on the way to the beach.
3 I will never forget *climbing* / *to climb* Everest. It was the ultimate experience.
4 Kathryn tried *climbing* / *to climb* Everest three times but never succeeded.
5 Dan stopped *studying* / *to study* after the exam.
6 They regretted *going* / *to go* to the party as they didn't know anyone and they felt awkward.
7 Dad tried *completing* / *to complete* the crossword but it was impossible.
8 I regret *informing* / *to inform* you that there are no places left on the course.

UNIT 2

that and *which* in relative clauses

Learners often use *that* instead of *which* in non-defining relative clauses.

✓ *Working leads to self-esteem, **which** is vital for most people.*
✗ *Working leads to self-esteem, ~~that~~ is vital for most people.*

Match the two parts of the sentences and rewrite them as one sentence using either *that* or *which*. Use *that* where possible.

0 The Arctic tern flies about 70,000 miles, [*b*]
1 The grey whale is the animal [ ]
2 Domenico Lucano had an idea [ ]
3 Our teacher always praises us when we've done well in a test, [ ]
4 I spoke to him using Italian, [ ]
5 Elena has decided to live abroad, [ ]

a helps give us confidence.
b is an amazing distance.
c swims about 18,000 km every year.
d I think is very brave of her.
e saved his village.
f I had learned while working there.

0 *The Arctic tern flies about 70,000 miles, which is an amazing distance.*

Relative pronouns

Learners often omit relative pronouns in defining relative clauses when you can't.

✓ *I don't know the number of people* ***who*** *went to the festival.*

✗ *I don't know the number of ~~people went~~ to the festival.*

Which of these sentences are correct and which are incorrect? Rewrite the incorrect ones.

0 Did you run into any of the people usually play there on Mondays?
Did you run into any of the people who usually play there on Mondays?

1 The pedestrians crossing the road had to run to avoid being hit by the car.
____

2 There was a food shortage caused by the extreme weather last summer.
____

3 They went through a bad time lasted a few months.
____

4 Who is the man waving at us?
____

5 Those are the residents live in that building over there.
____

6 The Bedouin are the people are always on the move.
____

UNIT 3

much vs. *many*

Learners often confuse *much* and *many*.

✓ *There are* ***many*** *more advantages than disadvantages.*

✗ *There are ~~much~~ more advantages than disadvantages.*

✓ *There was* ***much*** *more information on the website.*

✗ *There was ~~many~~ more information on the website.*

Complete the sentences with *much* or *many*.

1 There wouldn't be so __________ naughty children if parents were stricter.
2 I can spend as __________ time as necessary making the costume.
3 She should ask Mrs Davies for advice. She knows so __________ about parenting.
4 The book contains __________ useful ideas about bringing up children.
5 You should come inside now. You've already spent too __________ time in the sun.
6 There is __________ more to be said about this but we don't have time now.

much and *most*

A common error for learners is mistakes with *most* by preceding it with *the* or following it by *of* when this isn't necessary.

✓ ***Most*** *drivers are careless.*

✗ *~~The~~ most drivers are careless.*

✓ ***Most*** *parents find bringing up children a challenge.*

✗ *Most ~~of~~ parents find bringing up children a challenge.*

Tick (✓) the correct sentences and cross (✗) the incorrect ones. Then rewrite the incorrect sentences correctly.

1 The most of my teachers at school were quite strict. ☐
2 Most of my friends use their phones a lot. ☐
3 James spent most of the time I was there getting ready for the fancy-dress party. ☐
4 Sally tried on a few outfits but the most of them were too big for her. ☐
5 It would be interesting to know if most of people agreed with the strict new rules. ☐
6 Were the most of your old school friends at the reunion? ☐

UNIT 4
used to

Learners often make mistakes with *used to*, writing *use to* instead of *used to* and also using it to talk about present habits.

✓ *I **used** to help him when he was ill.*

✗ *I ~~use~~ to help him when he was ill.*

✓ *I **usually** go running twice a week if I have the time.*

✗ *I ~~use to~~ go running twice a week if I have the time.*

Rewrite these incorrect sentences correctly.

1 Liam use to be very bad-tempered but he's nicer now.
2 There's a lot of planning involved in my job, so I use to be organised.
3 When I was at school we use to sit in a row in some lessons.
4 They use to go to school by bus, except for Tuesdays when they walk.
5 The man who use to live there moved to Spain.
6 Sara used to watch a lot of TV when she hasn't got much homework.

UNIT 5
should

Learners often use *would* and *must* instead of *should*.

✓ *Lots of people think that animals **should** be free.*

✗ *Lots of people think that animals ~~must~~ be free.*

For each pair of sentences tick (✓) the correct one.

1 A ☐ Your computer is very slow. I think you should upgrade your system.
B ☐ Your computer is very slow. I think you must upgrade your system.

2 A ☐ Sophie wouldn't have emigrated if she hadn't been unhappy here.
B ☐ Sophie shouldn't have emigrated if she hadn't been unhappy here.

3 A ☐ Our teachers should motivate us to study more so we do better in exams.
B ☐ Our teachers would motivate us to study more so we do better in exams.

4 A ☐ We should launch the new product before the end of the month or we won't hit the sales figures. We have no other option.
B ☐ We must launch the new product before the end of the month or we won't hit the sales figures. We have no other option.

UNIT 6
Comparatives

Learners often use the comparative instead of the superlative and vice versa.

✓ *That was the **worst** evening of my holiday.*

✗ *That was the ~~worse~~ evening of my holiday.*

✓ *Their behaviour seems to getting **worse**.*

✗ *Their behaviour seems to getting ~~worst~~.*

Complete the sentences with the correct superlative or comparative in the list.

best | better | happier | happiest
harder | hardest | higher | highest

1 The ____________ the questions, the more money can be won by the participants.
2 What's the ____________ way to ask someone out?
3 When Liz got married, it was the ____________ day of her life.
4 The ____________ the salary, the more extra money to spend you have.
5 The exam I sat yesterday was the ____________ one I've ever done.
6 Luke and Molly's engagement party would have been ____________ if they'd invited more people.
7 Tom decided to climb the ____________ mountain in Scotland.
8 Some people think that the richer you are the ____________ you are.

Linkers of contrast

Learners often confuse linkers or make mistakes with form.

✓ ***Although** I studied a lot, I failed the exam.*

✗ *~~Despite~~ I studied a lot, I failed the exam.*

Rewrite the sentences either by using a different linker or by changing the form of the sentence.

0 In spite they got engaged, they never got married.
Although they got engaged, they never got married.
In spite of getting engaged, they never got married.
1 Even though confessing to the crime, the police didn't arrest her.
2 We made an enquiry about the delivery. Despite, no one got back to us.
3 Nevertheless the fact that they made a complaint about the food, the chef didn't apologise.
4 The children took the move to the countryside in their stride, despite they had been happy living in the city.

UNIT 7
Future continuous

Learners often use the present continuous when the future continuous is more commonly used.

✓ *On holiday we **will be staying** in tents.*
✗ *On holiday we ~~are staying~~ in tents.*

Tick (✓) the sentences which sound perfectly natural as they are and rewrite the other ones.

1 I'll see you tomorrow outside the hospital at 3 pm. ☐

______

2 I am seeing you sometime over the weekend, so I'll show you then. ☐

______

3 When we meet, I'll be wearing a black dress and a hat. ☐

______

4 I'll come to the airport to pick you up. I'm waiting for you at arrivals. ☐

______

5 Daphne won't come to the party on Saturday as she's busy. ☐

______

6 This time next week they will lie on a beach relaxing. ☐

______

UNIT 8
would

Learners often use *would* in the *if* clause of conditional sentences instead of using a present, past simple or past perfect form.

✓ *Don't hesitate to contact me if you **need** any more information.*
✗ *Don't hesitate to contact me if you ~~would~~ need any more information.*
✓ *If you **had come** to the park, you would have enjoyed yourself.*
✗ *If you ~~would have~~ come to the park, you would have enjoyed yourself.*

Put the words in order to make sentences. In each sentence there is an extra word that you don't need.

1 If / would / run through / the / mistake / calculations / they / they / would / have / realised / had / their / .

______

2 cookbook / The / wouldn't / meal / wouldn't / turned out / lent / so well / if / you / hadn't / me / have / your / .

______

3 would / 'll / that / She / do / her / provided / we / help / it / .

______

4 get / infection / you / hands, / might / don't / would / wash / If / your / you / an / .

______

5 The / wouldn't / been / have / ripped / would / it / had / cloth / if / stronger / .

______

6 as / time / won't / It / problem / long / a / as / would / arrive / on / be / you / .

______

UNIT 9
wish

Learners often use *wish* when *hope* or *want* are required and vice versa.

✓ *I **want** my children to live in a happy family.*
✗ *I ~~wish~~ my children to live in a happy family.*

Choose the correct verb.

1 Chloe *hopes / wishes* you hadn't told her about Toby.
2 I *wish / hope* you have a good time in Mallorca.
3 Dad *wishes / wants* to learn how to play the piano.
4 We *want / wish* our next-door neighbour didn't play the violin.
5 Francesco *hopes / wishes* to get on a degree course next year.
6 I *hope / wish* that the play lived up to your expectations.
7 I'm having a BBQ on Saturday and I *hope / wish* you can come.

wish / if only

Learners often use the past simple instead of the past perfect after *wish / if only* when talking about the past.

✓ *I wish I **had gone** to the party.*

✗ *I wish I ~~went~~ to the party.*

Match the two parts of the sentences.

1 I wish we won ☐
2 I wish we had won ☐
3 Max's mum wishes he had studied harder ☐
4 Max's mum wishes he studied harder ☐
5 If only I had slept until later ☐
6 If only I didn't sleep so late ☐
7 If only Jasper hadn't let you down ☐
8 If only Jasper didn't let you down ☐

a at school so he could get into university.
b all the time, you'd be friends.
c a match occasionally. It would be nice!
d I wouldn't be so tired now.
e you'd still be friends.
f the match. Everyone was so disappointed.
g at school and got into university.
h I'd have more time in the mornings.

UNIT 10
Reported speech

Learners often omit *if* when reporting *yes/no* questions, or use the auxiliary *do* when it isn't needed. Learners also need to be careful with word order in reported speech.

✓ *He asked me **if** I wanted to go.*

✗ *He asked me ~~did I want~~ to go.*

✓ *The teacher asked me how old **I was**.*

✗ *The teacher asked me how old ~~was I~~.*

Tick (✓) the correct sentences and rewrite the incorrect ones correctly.

1 Simon asked me did I remember to pass on the message to the class. ☐
2 He asked if he was in their way. ☐
3 Xenia asked how efficiently worked the machine. ☐
4 She asked could any politician ever be impartial. ☐
5 The students asked the speaker how big had been the impact of war. ☐
6 The chief editor asked the journalist if he did think the article was newsworthy. ☐

UNIT 11
Cause and effect linkers

Learners often make mistakes with cause and effect linkers: *so, consequently, because of, due to, as a result of*.

✓ *It's easier to go by train **because** you have no parking problems.*

✗ *It's easier to go by train ~~for~~ you have no parking problems.*

Choose the correct linker.

1 *Consequently / Due to / Because* the film's success, the director was in high demand.
2 Many people witnessed the solar eclipse. *So / Because of / As a result,* a number of people were admitted to hospital with eye damage.
3 It's a very popular tourist destination *because of / as a result / due* its breathtaking views.
4 Emily spent most of her money in the first week of her holiday and *because / consequently / as a result* had very little to spend in the second week.
5 I really hate being interrupted *because / so / consequently* please wait for me to finish speaking!
6 Daniela's dad was cross *as a result / for / because of* her disappointing exam results.

UNIT 12
been and *being*

Learners often confuse *been* and *being*.

✓ *I don't think your talent is **being** recognised.*

✗ *I don't think your talent is ~~been~~ recognised.*

✓ *I've always **been** able to rely on him.*

✗ *I've always ~~being~~ able to rely on him.*

Choose the correct form, *been* or *being*.

1 Work on the school is *being / been* carried out at the moment.
2 Advances are *being / been* made all the time in medical research.
3 Police have *being / been* trying to determine exactly what happened during the burglary.
4 Sebastian feels like he's *being / been* taken advantage of.
5 I remember *being / been* amazed at the size of the waterfall.
6 Since we played the joke on him, he's *being / been* avoiding us.

STUDENTS A & C

UNIT 6, PAGE 56

Student A
You are a real Comic Con fan. You spent hours designing and creating your costume and you had high hopes that you would win a prize. You are very upset as you know there's no time for you to create a costume that is anywhere near as good.

Student C
You had bought a costume from the local fancy dress store and being a practical kind of person, you'd spent a few hours adapting it to make it better. You are always good at coming up with good solutions to problems.

STUDENTS B & D

UNIT 6, PAGE 56

Student B
You are actually quite relieved. You're not really a fan of Comic Con anyway and only agreed to come to keep your best friend company. You had a cheap costume that you bought from a department store and you weren't particularly looking forward to wearing it.

Student D
You were going to Comic Con dressed as Sherlock Holmes. This is because you've always fancied yourself as a bit of an amateur detective. The missing suitcase has intrigued you and you want to find exactly what has happened to it, even if it means missing a bit of Comic Con.